# The Garland Library
# of Medieval Literature

### General Editors
James J. Wilhelm, Rutgers University
Lowry Nelson, Jr., Yale University

### Literary Advisors
Ingeborg Glier, Yale University
Guy Mermier, University of Michigan
Fred C. Robinson, Yale University
Aldo Scaglione, University of North Carolina

### Art Advisor
Elizabeth Parker McLachlan, Rutgers University

### Music Advisor
Hendrik van der Werf, Eastman School of Music

# Guillaume de Machaut

## The Judgment of the King of Bohemia
## (Le Jugement dou Roy de Behaingne)

edited and translated by
R. BARTON PALMER

Volume 9
Series A
GARLAND LIBRARY OF MEDIEVAL LITERATURE

Garland Publishing, Inc.
New York & London
*1984*

Library of Congress Cataloging in Publication Data

Guillaume, de Machaut, ca. 1300–1377.
The judgment of the King of Bohemia = Le jugement dou roy de Behaingne.
(Garland library of medieval literature ; v. 9. Series A)
Bibliography: p.
I. Palmer, R. Barton, 1946–    . II. Title.
III.   Title: Jugement dou roy de Behaingne.  IV. Series:
Garland library of medieval literature ; v. 9
PQ1483.G5A68   1984    841'.1    83-48241
ISBN 0-8240-9438-7

Printed on acid-free, 250-year-life paper
Manufactured in the United States

# The Garland Library
## of Medieval Literature

Series A (Texts and Translations); Series B (Translations Only)

1. Chrétien de Troyes: *Lancelot, or The Knight of the Cart*. Edited and translated by William W. Kibler. Series A.
2. Brunetto Latini: *Il Tesoretto*. Edited and translated by Julia Bolton Holloway. Series A.
3. *The Poetry of Arnaut Daniel*. Edited and translated by James J. Wilhelm. Series A.
4. *The Poetry of William VII, Count of Poitiers, IX Duke of Aquitaine*. Edited and translated by Gerald A. Bond. Series A.
5. *The Poetry of Cercamon and Jaufre Rudel*. Edited and translated by George Wolf and Roy Rosenstein. Series A.
6. *The Vidas of the Troubadours*. Translated by Margarita Egan. Series B.
7. *Medieval Latin Poems of Male Love and Friendship*. Translated by Thomas Stehling. Series A.
8. *Bárðar Saga*. Edited and translated by Jón Skaptason and Phillip Pulsiano. Series A.
9. Guillaume de Machaut: *Judgment of the King of Bohemia*. Edited and translated by R. Barton Palmer. Series A.
10. *Three Lives of the Last Englishmen*. Translated by Michael Swanton. Series B.
11. Giovanni Boccaccio: *The Elegy of Lady Fiammetta*. Translated by Mariangela Causa-Steindler. Series B.
12. Walter Burley: *On the Lives and Characters of the Philosophers*. Edited and translated by Paul Theiner. Series A.
13. *Waltharius* and *Ruodlieb*. Edited and translated by Dennis Kratz. Series A.
14. *The Writings of Medieval Women*. Translated by Marcelle Thiébaux. Series B.
15. *The Rise of Gawain (De Ortu Waluuani)*. Edited and translated by Mildred Day. Series A.

*v*

16, 17. *The French Fabliau*: Berne MS. (2 vols). Edited and translated by Raymond Eichmann and John DuVal.   Series A.

18. *The Poetry of Guido Cavalcanti*. Edited and translated by Lowry Nelson, Jr.   Series A.

19. Hartmann von Aue: *Iwein*. Edited and translated by Patrick M. McConeghy.   Series A.

20. *Seven Medieval Latin Comedies*. Translated by Alison Goddard Elliott.   Series B.

21. Christine de Pisan: *The Epistle of the Prison of Human Life*. Edited and translated by Josette Wisman.   Series A.

22. Marie de France: *Fables*. Edited and translated by Harriet Spiegel.   Series A.

23. *The Poetry of Cino da Pistoia*. Edited and translated by Christopher Kleinhenz.   Series A.

24. *The Lyrics and Melodies of Adam de la Halle*. Edited and translated by Deborah Nelson with music edited by Hendrik van der Werf.   Series A.

25. Chrétien de Troyes. *Erec and Enide*. Edited and translated by Carleton Carroll.   Series A.

26. *Three Ovidian Tales*. Edited and translated by Raymond J. Cormier.   Series A.

27. *The Poetry of Guido Guinizelli*. Edited and translated by Robert Edwards.   Series A.

28. Wernher der Gartenaere: *Meier Helmbrecht*. Translated by Linda B. Parshall; edited by Ulrich Seelbach.   Series A.

To my loving wife

# Preface of the General Editors

The Garland Library of Medieval Literature was established to make available to the general reader modern translations of texts in editions that conform to the highest academic standards. All of the translations are original, and were created especially for this series. The translations attempt to render the foreign works in a natural idiom that remains faithful to the originals.

The Library is divided into two sections: Series A, texts and translations; and Series B, translations alone. Those volumes containing texts have been prepared after consultation of the major previous editions and manuscripts. The aim in the editing has been to offer a reliable text with a minimum of editorial intervention. Significant variants accompany the original, and important problems are discussed in the Textual Notes. Volumes without texts contain translations based on the most scholarly texts available, which have been updated in terms of recent scholarship.

Most volumes contain Introductions with the following features: (1) a biography of the author or a discussion of the problem of authorship, with any pertinent historical or legendary information; (2) an objective discussion of the literary style of the original, emphasizing any individual features; (3) a consideration of sources for the work and its influence; and (4) a statement of the editorial policy for each edition and translation. There is also a Select Bibliography, which emphasizes recent criticism on the works. Critical writings are often accompanied by brief descriptions of their importance. Selective glossaries, indices, and footnotes are included where appropriate.

The Library covers a broad range of linguistic areas, including all of the major European languages. All of the important literary forms and genres are considered, sometimes in anthologies or selections.

The General Editors hope that these volumes will bring the general reader a closer awareness of a richly diversified area that has for too long been closed to everyone except those with precise academic training, an area that is well worth study and reflection.

James J. Wilhelm
*Rutgers University*

Lowry Nelson, Jr.
*Yale University*

# Contents

Introduction                                    xiii

Select Bibliography                             xliii

*The Judgment of the King of Bohemia*              1

Textual Notes                                    92

Chaucerian Parallel Passages                     97

# Introduction

## Life of the Author

Guillaume de Machaut was undoubtedly the most renowned and influential poet of fourteenth-century France. In large measure, his reputation resulted from his production of an immense and varied corpus of works, many of which were composed for the great nobles whom Machaut served as secretary and chaplain. As a musician, he wrote more than twenty motets and a polyphonic setting of the ordinary of the mass, the virtuosity and innovations of which earned him the admiration of his contemporaries. He also wrote a large body of lyric poems, in various fixed forms like the *ballade* and the *virelay*, and was responsible for the continuing fashion of this type of poetry (for further details see Poirion's work of 1965, details in Select Bibliography). Finally, following in the tradition of thirteenth-century love poetry, especially the *Romance of the Rose*, Machaut composed ten long narrative and didactic poems (*dits*) and four shorter ones. These not only pleased the noble audiences for which they were intended, but exerted considerable influence on poets to follow, particularly Jean Froissart, Eustache Deschamps, and Christine de Pizan, and also on the young Geoffrey Chaucer, particularly as evidenced in early poetry, such as *The Book of the Duchess*.

Because he was a low-born cleric, even though he was a servant of the well-born and famous, little is now known about Machaut's life, beyond what has been preserved in various ecclesiastical documents and what the poet reveals about himself in his own works, especially in the longer *dits*. From the later documents which detail his appointment to certain benefices, it can be inferred that Machaut was born at or near the beginning of the fourteenth century, probably in the village of Machault in Champagne (Ardennes). Since the same documents fail to qualify his name with the usual adjectives denoting noble rank, it can also be assumed that he was of humble origin. This social status is consistent with the self-portrait that emerges from the poetry itself, in which Machaut often makes his poetic *persona* a humble and cowardly clerk who moves somewhat uncertainly among his betters, the butt of class humor.

Many documents refer to Machaut as "master." This means that after an early education, probably in the cathedral school of Rheims, Machaut pursued theological studies at a university, possibly Paris. Though he received the Master of Arts degree, he did not go on to take Holy Orders, or so it can be assumed, since he is nowhere referred to as a priest and only served in the offices open to those outside the priesthood.

Instead his career took another direction, one that permitted low-born clerics, who, like himself, had the right education and the requisite social acumen, to advance in society. Through circumstances no longer known, Machaut, while in his early twenties, became associated with one of the most notable grand nobles of the era, John of Luxembourg, the King of Bohemia. To the modern historian John seems an extravagant and perhaps unstable figure; to his contemporaries, however, John's fabulous prodigality, his impractical military ventures, and his social finesse appeared to be the apotheosis of courtliness. For a number of years, Machaut served John as both secretary and chaplain (so ecclesiastical documents attest) and, according to Machaut's own testimony in *Le Confort d'Ami (Comfort for a Friend)*, accompanied him on several military expeditions to eastern Europe and elsewhere, the harrowing experiences of which Machaut relates in some detail. During the same period, through John's influence, Machaut came to hold a number of church offices, including that of canon at Rheims (in which he would continue until his death). John died at the Battle of Crécy (1346) in a final, magnificent gesture of military bravery, since he was blind at the time. It is uncertain, however, if Machaut was still closely associated with him then. He had probably left John's service before 1340, returning to his duties at Rheims, where he was to reside, except for occasional sojourns at other noble courts, for the rest of his life.

During his association with the King of Bohemia, Machaut began to establish a reputation for himself with both musical and poetical works. Three of his longer *dits* were certainly composed and circulated prior to 1342: *Dit dou vergier (The Story of the Garden)*, *Le Jugement dou Roy de Behaingne (The Judgment of the King of Bohemia)*, and *Remede de Fortune (Fortune's Remedy)*. Their success enabled Machaut to find other noble patrons after John's death.

In the years immediately following Crécy, Machaut apparently did not enter the service of John's son Charles, the Emperor of Germany. Much later, however (about 1370), Machaut did dedicate a narrative poem to him, the historical chronicle *La Prise d'Alexandrie (The Capture of Alexandria)*. For a time Machaut did become associated with John's daughter Bonne, the wife of Duke John of Normandy, but Bonne died in 1349.

During the plague year of 1348–49, Machaut took refuge behind cloister walls, as he recounts in great detail at the beginning of *Le Jugement dou Roy de Navarre (The Judgment of the King of Navarre)*, and he afterward entered the service of the monarch mentioned in the title, Charles the Bad. This relationship apparently continued for some time. When Charles was taken prisoner by the English in 1356 and held for two years, Machaut wrote *Comfort for a Friend* and sent it to Charles in an attempt to reconcile him to his captivity. The intimacy with which Machaut addresses Charles attests to a close personal relationship between them. This undoubtedly explains why Machaut's brother Jean also entered the king's service and was provided with the usual benefice.

Perhaps because of the hostilities that erupted between Charles and the Valois, Machaut left the court of Navarre not long after Charles' return from England. During the last years of his life, Machaut received the patronage of a number of the great lords of France, including King John the Good and his son John, the Duke of Berry. One of Machaut's most famous works, the *Dit de la fonteinne amoureuse (The Story of the Lovers' Fountain)*, is dedicated to the duke and features him as the main character.

Machaut died at Rheims in April of 1377, where he and his brother were eventually interred in the same cathedral grave. (For further details, see Machabey's biography of 1955, on whose work this brief account is based.)

# Artistic Achievement

After delivering a manuscript of Guillaume de Machaut's poetry to
Count Louis de Male of Flanders, Eustache Deschamps, Machaut's
disciple, dedicated a poem to his master in which he observes:

> All your works are with great honor
> Received by all in many a far-off place,
> And there no one, as far as I know,
> Speaks anything of them but your praises.
> Guillaume, the great lords hold you very dear,
> And take pleasure in what you write.
>
> (Text in Hoepffner, *Oeuvres*, I, iv)

Despite his close relationship to Machaut, we can without hesita-
tion accept Deschamps' judgment at face value. For, as we have
seen, Machaut enjoyed the patronage of some of the most impor-
tant nobles of his age, a privilege that, as Deschamps correctly
observes, depended on the poet's ability to please and entertain.

Moreover, Deschamps is not the only contemporary to speak
glowingly of Machaut's accomplishments. Numerous other
praiseworthy references prove that Deschamps echoes here what
must have been the received view of Machaut. Indirect, but cer-
tainly eloquent, testimony to Machaut's acclaim is also furnished
by the many beautiful surviving manuscripts of his works, some of
which were copied many years after his death. Finally, we can infer
that Machaut was highly regarded by the other great poets of his
age who, unlike Deschamps, left no recorded opinions on the sub-
ject. For Geoffrey Chaucer and Christine de Pizan especially, if they
did not acknowledge their admiration for the narrative poems, did
pay Machaut the sincere flattery of imitating and adapting them.

Today Machaut's musical innovations and virtuosity have
earned him a deservedly important place in the history of music.
His lyric poetry, because it codified and popularized different fixed
forms like the *virelay*, continues to be considered an important
element in the development of lyric types destined to flourish under
later poets, especially François Villon. Machaut's ten major *dits*,
however, including *The Judgment of the King of Bohemia*, have
until recently not fared well with modern critics. Thus any consider-
ation of the artistic value of the present poem must first confront, in

general terms, the entrenched critical disapproval of Machaut's work in the genre as a whole.

The reasons for this disapproval are easy to discover. Since it values highly both the "creative" artist and narrative fiction designed for realistic effect, much modern intrinsic criticism has signally failed to develop an appreciative approach to the narrative love poetry of the late French Middle Ages, which is often quite conventional (that is, not the product of originality in the modern sense) and also essentially unrealistic (that is, generally unconcerned with reproducing the feel of ordinary experience). Daniel Poirion's writings of 1965 and 1971 are notable exceptions, while recent work on Machaut's contemporaries likewise suggests a change in attitude. Since the Victorian era, the *dits amoreux* of Machaut, Deschamps, Froissart, and Christine de Pizan, among others, have been nearly unanimously dismissed as unoriginal reworkings of shopworn conventions. Considered as mere artifacts of a supposedly defunct literary tradition, this poetry has therefore been assigned a marginal place in literary history, as a series of footnotes to the great poetic accomplishments of the High Middle Ages or, at best, as a series of tentative steps away from the conventions of the past.

Machaut's *dits*, as a result, have been considered only in terms of their conventions (particularly narrative structures such as the dream vision and themes such as the "doctrines" of courtly love) and in terms of their violation of convention (the poet's attempts to escape the anxiety of influence, to render "realistically" both contemporary events and social practice). Ernest Hoepffner, Machaut's fullest editor and enthusiastic admirer, for example, finds it necessary to locate the poet's accomplishment in his search (albeit unsuccessful) for a style and content free from convention:

> For, if he found it impossible to extricate himself from the domination exerted by the *Romance of the Rose* over the era as a whole, he did however succeed in forging for himself a certain originality which belonged to him alone and for which he was indebted to no one else, in that he mixed elements completely personal and individual with fiction of an abstract and general kind.
>
> (*Oeuvres*, I, ii)

Hoepffner's observation about this poetic "mixture" is insightful and will be discussed at greater length below. For the moment, we may notice his determination to justify Machaut's achievement according to modern notions of "originality." This determination leads Hoepffner to what is certainly a grave error: the notion that Machaut viewed convention, the inheritance of a respected artistic past, as a domination to be overthrown.

Conceived in this way, Machaut's career has inevitably been measured against that of Geoffrey Chaucer, who in his early poetry manifests the substantial influence that Machaut's works exerted upon him. Chaucer, like Machaut, honored the poetic past and, not surprisingly, evidently considered himself to be working within a time-honored tradition. But there, according to the standard modern view, the resemblance between the two poets ends. Kittredge, like other early critics, maintained that Chaucer soon rejected the claims of traditional poetry in favor of a realistic treatment of experience (see especially *Chaucer and His Poetry*). According to this model, Machaut afforded the tradition that Chaucer wisely abandoned. Machaut's poetry, by comparison, becomes an uninteresting homage to Guillaume de Lorris, unswerving in its refusal of artistic freedom.

More recent views of Chaucer's career have wisely discarded Kittredge's contrast between the periods of conventionalism and realism. Some years ago, Charles Muscatine demonstrated that, while the later works are also conventional, they are more successful because they are structured around the interplay of discourses, in particular those of classic courtly idealism and *fabliaux* realism. Within this mode, still the consensus among Chaucerians, Machaut also turns out to be an artistic failure because of his purported inability to derive a meaningful effect from his own efforts to mix discourses. Muscatine terms this his "peculiar linkage of convention and realism" (p. 100). According to Muscatine, Machaut's mixture of discourses is peculiar in its "artificiality" because it fails to evoke the experience of felt life. Judged by these canons of modern criticism, Machaut's narrative poetry will inevitably be found wanting, an unsuccessful attempt to achieve the richness and originality of his English counterpart.

But the canons of modern criticism were hardly the aims of poetry as Machaut understood them. We are, as it happens, in a position to judge these rather directly. For, in the long *Prologue* composed as an introduction to a collected edition of his works, Machaut has left us very explicit testimony about his conception of the poet. There are signs, moreover, that a more historically based criticism of Machaut's poetry is developing (see the essays by Uitti, Brownlee, and Manley Williams in Cosman and Chandler, all of which take into account the importance of the *Prologue*). Building upon this critical work, one can analyze the *Prologue* as an expression of the poet's attempt to position himself within the discourse of the love poetry, whose influence he felt very strongly.

Machaut took a continuing interest in the form and reception of his works, much more so than many of his contemporaries. In the autobiographical *Voir Dit (True Story)*, he declares that he kept a comprehensive exemplar of his works with him at all times: "the book where I put all I've done." The textual history of the poems themselves, moreover, demonstrates that Machaut, apparently often dissatisfied with the original versions, revised them. The last versions of *The Judgment of the King of Bohemia*, for example, which are preserved in the great cyclical manuscripts copied (perhaps under the poet's supervision) toward the end of his life, lack four passages (lines 980–83; 1000–47; 1816–19; and 1861–84 in the present edition), which can be found in earlier versions. The excision of these passages cannot be accounted for by ordinary processes of textual revision or scribal redaction, and must then be the result of the poet's revision (see Manley Williams 1969 1978 for further discussion along these lines). In addition, Manuscript A, a direct descendant of what was probably the final version of Machaut's corpus, contains a most unusual heading over its index of contents that likewise testifies to the poet's interest in the circulated form of his compositions: "Here follows the order of works which G. de Machaut wishes there to be in his book" (Vesci l'ordenance que G. de Machau vuet quil ait en son livre). Because of Machaut's substantial concern about the reception of his work, it is therefore hardly surprising that, toward the end of his career, he composed a prologue to explain why he wrote love poetry and to account for the content and form of the different poems themselves.

The 298-line *Prologue* is divided into five sections, the first four of which are cast in the form of *ballades*, while the last is written in rhymed couplets. The first two *ballades* comprise a dialogue between the poet and Lady Nature, while the others are devoted to a dialogue between the poet and Love. The poem concludes with the poet's meditations about the craft into which he is about to enter. A prose heading explains that Lady Nature, "wishing more than ever before to reveal and exalt the goods and honor which are in Love, comes to Guillaume de Machaut and orders him to create these new poems about love." Nature then addresses the poet directly:

> I, Nature, by whom all things take form,
> All that there is above and on the earth and in the sea,
> Appear to you, Guillaume, whom I have formed
> For my part, in order to have formed by you
> New, pleasant poems about love.
> (I, lines 1-5, from Hoepffner, *Oeuvres*, I, 1)

This process of creation, however, requires more than a simple command. Nature introduces to Guillaume her three children: Meaning, Rhetoric, and Music, who will supply him with the intellectual and technical resources for the composition of verse, both lyrical and narrative. In closing, Nature predicts to Guillaume that "your works will be more renowned than those of any other, and there will be nothing in them to blame, and thus you'll be loved by all" (I, lines 19–21). Guillaume agrees to Nature's request, saying that he would hardly dare to refuse the one to whom he owes "body, life, and understanding." He adds humbly that he would never be able to bring such "great work" to fruition, were it not for the continuing presence and guidance of Nature's three children.

At this point Nature departs, and another prose heading informs us that Love, having overheard her request, has decided to appear to Guillaume and make him the gift of her three children: Sweet Thought, Pleasure, and Hope, who together will be able to furnish him with the content of the poetry Nature has charged him with writing. Love carefully warns Guillaume to observe the decorum of the love experience:

> But take care, above all else, that you are not emboldened
> To compose anything in which there's any rudeness,
> And never slander any of my ladies.
> But in every case praise and exalt them.
> Know well, that if you do the contrary,
> I will most cruelly deny you.
> Instead, do everything in honor and thus advance yourself.
> (III, lines 21–27)

Guillaume, once again humbly, agrees to Love's requests, observing that "never has a lover, however much he loved you, served you better than will I, according to my strength, as long as I will live." The *Prologue* then closes with Guillaume's meditations on the duty of the poet, in particular the necessity to compose with a happy heart, for the love experience brings the poet joy, and he must use his gifts to bring comfort to those who are sad.

The *Prologue* invites several readings, which reflect its function as offering both narrative fiction and an explanation for the real Guillaume's creative avocation. Within the fiction itself, Guillaume represents his creative persona in strictly conventional terms, that is, as a subject activated by the call, empowered by traditional skills and ideas, situated within a context of writing, and charged with a duty carefully defined by the hierarchies of creation in its several senses. The two dialogues, of course, are also conventional to the degree that they consciously align themselves with both religious and literary figures. Receiving the commandments of both Nature and Love, Guillaume finds himself constituted in the way medieval Christianity maintained that every individual was constituted: as created but also creating, as effected but also responsible. The scene is resonant, however, not only with religious values in general (with the biblical figure of the "call" in particular), but also with the many similar scenes from traditional love poetry where the archetypal lover is situated by allegorical characters, representatives of the principles of human experience and the universals of psychology. Traditionally, their functioning is associated, as here, with the "forming" that releases the lover to act.

Viewed as an explanation of Guillaume's historical situation, of course, the two dialogues invite a different reading. So viewed, the "call" becomes not only a natural experience, a means of representing with traditional allegorical machinery the internal workings of genius or talent, but also a way, through metaphor, of understanding Guillaume's relationship to his patrons.

Privileged by his education (the three gifts of Nature are a kind of artistic trivium), Guillaume undertakes the duty to write poetry; thus he receives the opportunity to surpass the work of others and to advance himself. But such a task means that he must have access to the kind of emotional experience ordinarily denied him by his class. Thus Love gives him emotional idealism as it is manifested in the three principal states that control it. In this reading, the gifts of

Nature and Love also constitute ways of viewing literary tradition—not, of course, as we normally (and perhaps distortingly) do as a series of texts, but rather as those rhetorical and thematic structurings which are the grounds of love poetry as a genre. Accepting those gifts, Machaut accepts the regulation of both narrative and theme made explicit by Love in her instructions. Only by this acceptance, Guillaume admits to both Love and Nature, can he even contemplate such a creative enterprise. Thus literary tradition dictates to the poet, demanding not the re-presentation of experience but the continued production of texts. These are to be judged, Machaut implies, only by their conformity to accepted rhetoric and the "truths" of love doctrine, not by originality or realism in the modern senses.

The *Prologue* thus expresses Machaut's view of the poet as a constituted subject, the servant of Nature and Love, as well as of his patrons. But the tradition of love poetry demanded the poet's subjectiveness in another sense, as the source of emotional truth; his represented persona is the rhetorical guarantee of the poem's claims to inform and comfort. It would be a mistake, however, to understand the poet's different roles as a subject simply in terms of genre. Machaut's works, in any case, permit no such easy division, since the narrative poems are also always lyrical to some extent, either because of the presence of lyric set pieces or because of the use of fixed stanzaic forms. The *Prologue* itself also gives us a sense of what Poirion has termed the "ambiguous I" of Machaut's poetry as a whole, the interplay between the discourses of the self and of tradition. For Love, in granting Machaut access to an experience restricted to members of the noble classes, grants him not knowledge of, but knowledge through, such an experience. Guillaume's promise to serve Love "better than any lover" and the figural significance of the scene itself (which deliberately echoes other interviews between the lover and the God of Love) both demonstrate that the command to produce love poetry involves the constitution of the poet himself as lover.

Such a meaning becomes perhaps most explicit in the *True Story*, where Guillaume himself, not just his abstract and familiar persona, becomes the subject of the love experience, which is "true" in the sense of being depicted without the usual mediating discourse of what Hoepffner terms the "abstract and general fiction" of this poetic tradition. In the other poems as well, we sense the effect of this "ambiguous I," the interplay between the poet's effacement behind the structuring givens of literary tradition and his simultaneous assertion of his own importance as an experiencing subject, the servant who writes from within and is not simply written by such poetry. This does not mean, however, as Hoepffner suggests, that we can imagine Machaut's career as an attempt to escape conventional fiction in its abstractness and, for traditional allegorical discourse, to substitute an original examination of subjective experience. Machaut's poetry is thoroughly conventional, for the contradictory senses of the poet's role are equally a part of this literary tradition. Machaut's "originality" paradoxically must include a thoroughgoing conventionalness. With this in mind, we can turn to an examination of *The Judgment of the King of Bohemia*, the poem of Machaut's most valued by his contemporaries, to judge from its influence on poets to follow and from its manuscript tradition (it is the only Machaut narrative poem to be found in manuscripts outside those devoted exclusively to the poet's works).

The poem opens with the narrator's reminiscences about a late April morning, the time appointed by Nature and God (it is the Easter season) for love. Love, he says, is an emotional experience that affects many men and women and brings them both joy and pain. This narrator, we learn, is an experienced and successful lover and therefore can give himself over quite happily to the enjoyment of the beautiful sunshine and a reawakening nature. Dressing as befits his station, he wanders out into the warm and clear air, and takes pleasure in the birdsong he hears. Following a nightingale, he enters a lonely glade, there to contemplate in solitude the indescribable beauty of the natural music he is listening to.

This short opening passage (lines 1–40) draws explicitly on the *Romance of the Rose*, in which the archetypal Amant (Lover) similarly falls prey to the enticements of springtime, falls asleep, and experiences a vision of the garden of Love where the poem's allegorical drama unfolds. In his first narrative poem, *The Story of the Garden*, Machaut had already drawn on these conventional structures and themes. In that earlier poem, however, the lover (unidentified as either clerk or poet) falls asleep after entering the garden and hearing the birds sing. Like Guillaume's Amant, he then has a vision of the God of Love, who instructs him in the experience of love. The opening of *The Judgment of the King of Bohemia* promises a similar narrative structure, but the poem takes a very different direction as it abandons the narrator as a focused character.

Instead of falling asleep and providing the arena for psychological allegory, the narrator becomes a witness to a drama that unfolds nearby. He sees a lady and a serving-girl approach down a lonely path; the lady seems very troubled. At the same moment, on the other side, he sees a knight approach. The two cross paths and, although the knight salutes the lady with proper courtesy, she ignores him. Puzzled, he takes the hem of her robe and questions her. The lady then confesses to being lost in thought because of the troubles that oppress her. The knight, like a true gentleman, offers his assistance, but is refused, since, as the lady declares, her difficulties are so severe that no one, save God, could alleviate either them or the pain they cause. The knight responds that he is suffering even more intensely, more than any human being ever has or could. This disagreement then leads naturally and quickly to a joint undertaking; the lady and knight will each confess their troubles in full so that it can be determined which one bears the greater burden of grief.

In lines 41 to 124, Machaut radically shifts the meaning of the narrator's solitude. At first it expresses his openness to the love experience, which is the result of his chance following the nightingale to a deserted spot, a stock motif. Suddenly that solitude, however, becomes the sign of his displacement from the narrative. Hidden in the brush, he becomes the witness of the debate between the knight and the lady; in these new circumstances, he remains the narrator but no longer serves as the subject of the narration. The poem itself, at first apparently a love vision, becomes a dispute over a question of love.

William Calin (1978) has suggested that this radical alteration in the poem's structure can be explained by Machaut's Jamesian discovery that a lack of distancing between the narrating-I and the experiencing-I made difficulties in focusing and verisimilitude. Yet it seems that if Machaut was dissatisfied with the identity between the narrating-I and the experiencing-I (which he borrows, with some modification, from Guillaume de Lorris), he would have begun the poem with this new technique instead of introducing it in a shocking way at this juncture. Machaut was too consummate a craftsman to create such a juxtaposition without carefully measuring its effect.

In love-debate poetry, the narrator ordinarily functions as no more than a "claim" for the fictional event's authenticity when he appears within the fiction at all. Machaut's use of his persona, however, is more complex. In most of his narrative poems, the persona performs a function within the fictional event that is somewhat analogous to the poet's functioning in his historical situation. Thus in the *Story of the Lovers' Fountain*, the poet-narrator diligently copies down the lyrical outburst he hears issuing from a nobleman's bedroom next door. Later, he provides the nobleman with this text of his own experience, and it is the textualizing process which permits both the narrator and the noble to fall asleep and receive the instructions of Venus (which are different because one is a clerk and the other a lover). In the present work the narrator, seemingly displaced from the center of the action, is not reduced to becoming a mere device. He remains, in an important sense, the master of ceremonies, controlling the progress of the action at a vital point.

The lady reveals her dedication to Love and her relationship with a knight who, in her view, was the best man of all. His death, she maintains, has left her with an irremediable sorrow, the proof of which seems to be the dead faint she falls into at the end of her speech (lines 125–205). After reviving her, the knight, however, does not agree, and in a lengthy response, (lines 260–860) describes his service to the God of Love, the reward he received of a young girl's heart, and the grief he suffers because she abandoned him for another. The lady, though sympathetic with his plight, still does not agree that his is the greater grief. She argues that, since his beloved is still living, it is possible for him to regain her favor through loyal and patient service. In his rebuttal, however, the knight maintains the contrary: if she were dead, he could forget her and be released from pain, but, being alive and forever unattainable, she will remain a continuing source of suffering for him. Thus the two disputants reach an impasse. Obviously they need a judge to decide the case, but, constrained by the rules of polite intercourse, neither wishes to nominate one.

Nearly forgotten during the progress of the debate, the narrator once again assumes a prominent (if different) role. At first the subject of the narrative, then the guarantor of its authenticity, he now becomes its prime mover. Like the disputants, the narrator finds himself in a difficult position, for, though he wishes to help them find a proper judge, he cannot reveal his presence for reasons of politeness. Chance, however, intervenes. The lady's dog spies him in the brush and runs toward him barking. The narrator picks him up and thus gains the opportunity to speak to the lady and knight without intruding himself. Confessing that he has heard all of their discussion, the narrator proposes the King of Bohemia as a judge to hear their case. They concur, and the narrator then becomes their guide to the nearby castle of Durbuy, where the king is in residence.

Once there, the narrator introduces the pair to the king, who graciously accepts to judge their dispute. He turns the matter over to his court for discussion and charges his various courtiers, who are allegorical personages such as Reason, Love, Youth, and Courtesy, with the explication of the issues involved. In a long response (lines 1665–1784), Reason confirms the correctness of the knight's arguments, maintaining that, since love is a carnal affection, it cannot survive the death of the body. Because her lover has died, the lady will eventually forget him. But the knight sees his unfaithful lady continually and cannot forget, even though Reason so advises, because Youth and Love urge him on in this mad error. Love herself then speaks, agreeing with Reason's solution of the dispute, but challenging her view that the knight should abandon his beloved because of her treason toward him. Rushing to Reason's support, Loyalty declares that the knight would not offend her if he should abandon the lady. Finally Youth joins the debate and asserts that the knight will never give up his love as long as her power can prevent it. The king gently reproves her, saying that she would overtax him with suffering and then concurs with Reason's judgment of the case, to which the other courtiers all assent. Offering his hospitality to the guests, the king keeps them for eight days, during which he does his best to comfort them in their sorrow and finally allows them to leave after giving them generous gifts. The poem closes with the poet's declaration of love for a lady from whom he has always expected only the simplest of rewards.

As was suggested earlier, an important value of *The Judgment of the King of Bohemia* lies in its reflexivity, particularly in its self-consciousness about the poet's working relationship to the structuring principles of literary tradition. It is likely, of course, that the poem's original audience might have prized it more for its competent organization and articulation of love poetry conventions: the *finesse* of its love doctrine, the liveliness of its allegorical characters, the sparkling set pieces, especially the knight's detailed evocation of his lady's appearance, the well-handled homage to John's notable qualities, and the realistic touches, like the role of the little dog, which lend authenticity to the traditionally abstract *mise-en-scène*. Well-versed in love poetry, that same audience, however, could hardly have overlooked those features which continually call attention to the poem's status as fiction and to the narrator-poet's role in its creation: the linkage of representational and abstract discourses in the portrait of John's court, the different relationships of the narrator to the experiences he relates, the humor with which the extreme doctrines of the love religion are subtly undermined, and the two passages (lines 1594–96 and 1781–84) in which characters refer to the poem's dialogue as contained in a text. To locate the poem's value solely in its poetic conventions is therefore surely to diminish the poet's accomplishments.

For Machaut sets out deliberately not only to compose a pleasing fiction but also to make his audience aware of the story's fictionalness and the poet's role in its making. One way to read the poem is to see it as an exploration of Machaut's uncertainties about his own position—as clerk and commoner, but also the designated voice of emotional idealism. Granted access to the direct experience of love, he discovers that the goal of that access is to write for his patrons, for the nobility as an institution. He abandons the combination of narrating-I and experiencing-I which he borrowed from Guillaume de Lorris not for technical reasons alone, but because he realizes that such a narrative viewpoint is inadequate to his historical situation as court poet.

Giving way to the concerns of the class he serves, he is still not content to be a simple witness, serving a narrating function that effaces itself behind the discourse. The role he fulfills is a larger one, for the poet, as Machaut sees it, is also a guide. His fictions are not just entertainments but rhetoric intended to inform and comfort. If his experience in love must be denied the privilege of narrative focus (must, in fact, be demonstrated to lead directly away from subjectivity), his duties as teacher and advisor cannot be so easily laid aside. In his later *dits*, especially *Fortune's Remedy*, Machaut attempts to infuse the traditional treatment of love with a Boethian idealism, with a sense of the serenity that comes with a disdain for the vagaries of individual misfortune. Thus it is hardly surprising that Machaut, as poetic master of ceremonies, allows the discussion of a love question in this early poem to turn toward another and more serious issue: the reconciliation of emotional release (represented by Youth) to intellectual understanding (represented by Reason). In this "digression" we sense not only Machaut's first attempts to come to grips with a matter raised in more detail by both Jean de Meun and Guillaume de Lorris, but also his conception of the poet's function diverting and, briefly, controlling the matter at hand. This issue vitally concerned him, as his later poems suggest, probably because it was so concerned with the poet's role as structured by tradition. For the *Romance of the Rose*, particularly the second part, embodies the split between the poet's persona as an actor in the drama of love and the implied author's wry condemnation of much that pertains to that drama. In *The Judgment of the King of Bohemia* the narrator's uncritical acceptance of love as an emotional state characterized by both joy and sorrow similarly contrasts with the poet's sympathetic portrait of Reason (who advocates emotional temperance) and his search beyond the superficial casuistry of the debate for an answer to a more fundamental question.

Though the poem in these ways takes as its subject the poet's role, that issue is hardly resolved in any final sense. Machaut must have viewed the regulating force of tradition as offering a number of positions which the author, as creator of the text and creature of such poetry, could occupy. In the *dits* to follow Machaut would use his persona in a number of ways: as the source of the love experience, as a comic butt against which the virtues of the nobility appear even more virtuous, as an instructor in moral wisdom, as a romance hero in search of adventure, and as an epic chronicler.

It is this experimentation and variety that finally distinguish his work from that of his predecessors, especially Guillaume de Lorris, and that of the love poets like Froissart and Deschamps, who otherwise followed him in so much else. Only Geoffrey Chaucer, as we shall see below, successfully imitated (and in some senses improved upon) the device of a narrator who could serve within the fiction as an expression of the author's attitude toward his material. Machaut's career must be understood as a continuing search for the connections among authorship, text, and audience, for the links and incongruities between an imaginary world shaped by Meaning, Rhetoric, and Music and the real world of social hierarchy, literary tradition, and emotional aspiration. Within that search, *The Judgment of the King of Bohemia* must be considered an important early step.

## Sources and Influences

In the preceding discussion, there was an occasion to note an interdependency of works within the genre of narrative love poetry. Machaut's borrowings from the *Romance of the Rose* are, of course, many and obvious. These indicate not Machaut's inability to go beyond the mastery of that popular model but rather his desire to anchor the meaning of the present poem to a solid and richly signifying base. Machaut insists that we read *The Judgment of the King of Bohemia* through the *Romance of the Rose*. The scope of his "quotations" from Guillaume de Lorris and Jean de Meun has been much discussed (see Robertson 1962; Calin 1974, 1978, 1979; Pelen 1976, and, most comprehensively, Kelly 1978). These influences include the spring-morning setting, replete with bird choruses, fair weather, and profuse flowers; the first-person narrator, who relates the adventures of his experiencing alter ego on that morning; the eventual journey to a Court of Love, where allegorical characters debate and explicate the intricate mysteries of love; and the stages of that experience evoked by the reminiscences of both the knight and the lady.

Yet it is important to emphasize that Machaut creates a very different kind of poem from these borrowings. For the opening section, where the "derivativeness" is most obvious, gives rise to the expectation that a dream vision will follow. The violation of that expectation constitutes, in effect, a statement that the poet will not follow further the narrative structure of that model but will turn toward a genre, the love debate, which was subsumed within (and superseded by) the *Romance of the Rose* (see Langlois 1890 for full details of this development). Machaut's handling of the other borrowings achieves much the same effect. The narratives of the knight's and lady's love affairs are embedded within the containing structures of the debate. Thus Machaut relates the love experience to a larger question, the sources of human happiness, whose discussion leads, perhaps inevitably, to the unresolved conflict between Reason and Loyalty on the one hand and Love and Youth on the other. As Kelly (1978) has demonstrated, Machaut's poetic career can be seen as a continuing attempt to synthesize the dictates of *fin'amors* (courtly love) with the philosophical perspectives of Boethius. Kelly points out that this synthesis is most obvious in the rhetorical stance of the later poems. We can, however, trace its beginnings in *The Judgment of the King of Bohemia* which, perhaps even more than Jean de Meun's continuation of Guillaume de Lorris, problematizes the love experience, transforming it into an issue that demands not the poet's subjectivity but rather his guidance.

Similarly motivated is an oft-remarked feature of the poem: the linkage of realistic and allegorical discourses in the presentation of John's court. As was suggested earlier, the *Prologue* forces us to reject Hoepffner's notion that Machaut attempted to escape from the domination of the *Romance of the Rose* and turn the traditional abstractness of love-vision poetry toward the presentation of personal experience. Therefore we cannot see the mixed discourses that constitute the Court of Love as a failed attempt to accomplish this goal, nor can we see this part of the poem as the French poet's lack of artistry preventing him from achieving the more subtle and seamless effects of Chaucer. The device of the little dog demonstrates that Machaut was certainly capable of reconciling verisimilitude and traditional fictional structures when this suited his purpose.

In his handling of the Court of Love, Machaut appears to reject such a reconciliation. For the effect of his mixture of discourses is to undermine any representational qualities the scene might have, to reduce it to its purely fictional (and hence rhetorical) essentials. John and his allegorical courtiers assume much the same status as intellectual and moral ciphers in the working out of the questions which the poem poses about the nature of love. But the location of the traditional Court of Love has another, and complementary, effect. This violation of the separation between waking and dreaming, the two levels of experience established by Guillaume de Lorris, collapses the distance between the individual search for emotional fulfillment and the abstract, collective truths of emotional idealism. Machaut, in other words, in this way presents us with an idealism available to the active, experiencing self, an idealism that can be located in the waking world directly and not figurally (for further discussion of these issues see Kelly 1978 and Palmer 1980, 1981). In sum, Machaut's borrowings from the *Romance of the Rose* are not indications of the poet's domination by tradition but rather of his desire to work within the meanings established by tradition, inventing the same ways to say other things. (See Peter Haidu 1974 for an interesting discussion of this issue in regard to medieval literature more generally.)

The relationship of *The Judgment of the King of Bohemia* to the love debate genre, however, must be approached differently. If Machaut counted on his audience recognizing his allusions to the *Romance of the Rose*, he could not do so in regard to the predecessors in the love debate genre which he in some sense drew upon, since these poems never achieved the same popularity and belonged largely to a much earlier age. As a result, these works are much less important for an understanding of the meaning of Machaut's poem. Debate poetry in the vernacular languages derives from a long-established, learned Latin tradition. Virgil's third, so-called "contention" eclogue inspired a host of late Latin imitations; the genre achieved particular popularity during the Carolingian revival (for a full account see Walther 1920). Of more interest than these rather dry arguments between roses and lilies or water and wine over relative merits, however, is the *Council of Remiremont*, a Latin poem that was probably written during the early years of the twelfth century. It features a lively and rather irreverent debate over the merits of clerks and knights as lovers; the debate takes place in the abbey of Remiremont, and the disputants are all nuns of the establishment. The poem achieved a good deal of popularity, if we may judge from the number of French imitations it spawned (the complex interrelationships of these are discussed by Jung 1971 and Langlois 1890; for texts see Oulmont 1911). These all feature the same subject of debate but alter the setting of the Latin poem and reduce the debaters to two women, one of whom loves a clerk and the other a knight.

The interest for us of these rather unaccomplished efforts lies in what, by contrast, they reveal about the complexity of Machaut's structuring of the debate in *The Judgment of the King of Bohemia*. For in none of these works do we find a narrator who, in addition to overhearing the debate, takes an active part in its resolution, leading the disputants to a judge who can settle their argument; nor in any of them does the scene of judgment itself become a further debate, in which the issue at hand broadens to encompass a fundamental examination of the love experience. Ultimately, then, Machaut's poem has little in common with the vernacular descendants of the *Council of Remiremont* beyond some obvious structural affinities.

Machaut's modification of love-vision narrative in *The Judgment of the King of Bohemia* affected later writers. Machaut himself was inspired by his evident success to produce a sequel, *The Judgment of the King of Navarre*, which, in a somewhat more elaborate fashion, continues the debate and reverses the King of Bohemia's decision. Also noteworthy is *Le Livre du dit de Poissy*, composed by Christine de Pizan in the early years of the fifteenth century (for a full discussion of the relationship between the two works see Schilperoort 1936). Pizan's imitation is, in many respects, a close one. Like Machaut, Pizan places her debate between a squire and a lady who are both suffering from different types of love distress not in a generalized *locus amoenus* but in an idealized representation of the "real" world. In *The Judgment of the King of Bohemia* the apparent universality of the orchard where the debate begins proves illusory. With the narrator's intervention, we learn that the drama is unfolding near Durbuy Castle, one of John's favorite residences, lovingly described with much detail by the narrator (lines 1384–1422). Pizan's poem opens with the narrator's extended description of the journey she made with a company of other ladies and gentlemen to the convent of Poissy not far from Paris. It is on the trip back from Poissy in the second half of the work that the debate between the squire and lady takes place.

The debate itself concerns a familiar subject. The lady confesses that she is in love with the best knight who has ever lived. After a detailed description of their love affair (which features a full account of her lover's appearance), she reveals that he has been taken prisoner in the military disaster at Nicopolis and been held for an exorbitant ransom by the Turks. Therefore she thinks never to see him again and suffers continual anguish for this reason. Though acknowledging that the lady has much cause for mourning, the squire declares that his pain is greater. After falling in love with a beautiful lady (who also is described with a conventional wealth of detail), he dedicated himself to her service, even soldiering abroad in an attempt to make himself worthy of her affection. On his return, however, she seemed cold. Puzzled by this indifference, he declared his love for her, asking for an explanation, but she rebuffed him, stating that no matter what service he performed, she would never change in her feelings. Recalling the argumentative strategy of her exemplar in Machaut's poem, the lady dismisses the squire's point that he suffers more because he lacks his lady's love and declares that, since he can still see her, he must have hope of winning her favor. Replying that he has none, that the sight of his beloved only increases his agony, the squire counters by affirming that the lady's knight will soon be released and that, in any case, she suffers less because she cannot see him. She naturally maintains the contrary and suggests that they seek a judge. The narrator obliges and nominates her patron, the nobleman to whom the poem itself is addressed, John of Hainaut.

At this point Pizan enlarges interestingly on the rhetorical structure of her source. For in Machaut's poem the interrogation of the love experience confines itself to the fictional setting and its characters. The narrator delivers the disputants to an imaginary rendering of John and his court, where the issue is decided. The *Dit de Poissy*, on the other hand, contains in its opening lines an appeal for the rendering of a judgment. Toward the end of the poem this appeal is repeated:

> They begged me to write this case up properly
> To send to you as soon as possible
> So that you could properly judge
> Which one truly bears the lighter burden
>> (Text in Roy 1891; lines 2046–49)

The result is a text that not only deals with interrogation but is itself formally interrogative.

Though, as his borrowings indicate, Geoffrey Chaucer depended on Machaut's poetry for its appropriate expression of conventional themes, the English poet was also influenced by the rhetoric of the poetry (see Calin 1974, 1978 and Palmer 1980 for further discussion). Much discussed, in particular, has been the narrator-dreamer of the *Book of the Duchess*, whose incurable lovesickness seems inspired by Froissart, but whose humorously delineated naiveté derives in some sense from Machaut's *The Judgment of the King of Bohemia* and *Story of the Lovers' Fountain* (the fullest discussion of the poem's intertextuality can be found in Wimsatt 1968 and Pelen 1976). While the direct borrowings have been discussed in some detail (especially by Kittredge in his *PMLA* article of 1915), treatment of larger structural similarities between the two poems has been largely confined to the character of the narrator, since Chaucer's poem, a dream vision, shares much more in common with Machaut's later *Story of the Lovers' Fountain*, which is also a dream vision. Therefore we need say no more here than that much of the dialogue between the dreamer and the Man in Black in the *Book of the Duchess* is rather closely adapted from the present poem (for the reader's convenience in assessing these borrowings I have printed the most important passages from Chaucer's poem as an appendix to the present edition). What has been largely passed over is Chaucer's handling of the narrator's relationship to literary tradition, which is also a central characteristic of *The Judgment of the King of Bohemia*.

In the *Book of the Duchess* the narrator's insomnia leads him to search out some reading that will help him sleep. Coming across the story of Ceyx and Alcyone, he thinks it a strange tale:

> For I had never herd speke, or tho,
> Of noo goddes that koude make
> Men to slepe, ne for to wake;
> For I ne knew never god but oon.
> (lines 234–47; text from Robinson 1957)

The tale itself, of course, derives largely from Machaut's *Story of the Lovers' Fountain*, where a sorrowing nobleman generates it spontaneously in his reaction to love-sorrow. Chaucer, however, turns the tale into a text which is problematically embedded within the narrator's account of his own experiences. For the narrator refuses any mythographic or metaphorical reading. Instead he scrutinizes what he reads historically; and he finds that the story leads him away from his own experience, with the dispensation of Christ, to a world that recognizes only the limited metaphysic of nature:

> And in this bok were written fables
> That clerkes had in olde tyme,
> And other poets, put in rime
> To rede, and for to be in minde,
> While men loved the lawe of kinde.

> (lines 62–66)

Thus the story exemplifies a literary tradition that does not reflect some of the narrator's basic assumptions. As he sees it, the underlying principle of tradition is natural love. By making us aware of the difference between experience and "auctoritee," the narrator communicates his hesitancy about taking a literary text too seriously, as a vehicle of truth.

Chaucer, to be sure, is having fun with the narrator's excessive literalness. Unlike sophisticated readers, he seems unable to suspend willingly his disbelief. But a more serious point is being made here as well. For if we understand the narrator in the tradition of Machaut's poetry as in some sense a fictionalization of the poet's historical situation, then the frame of Chaucer's poem presents the poet at work exploring the possibilities of using a literary tradition. As in *The Judgment of the King of Bohemia*, such an exploration occurs within the context of the narrator's search for release (which we may understand, extratextually, as the poet's search for what might comfort John of Gaunt, his sorrowing patron). I have maintained in some detail elsewhere (1980) that Chaucer's retelling of the story of Ceyx and Alcyone is problematical in its relevance to the assuaging of grief, for Chaucer excises the closing metamorphosis (in which both lovers, turned into birds, are eternally reunited, the symbol for Machaut of love's power to overcome Fortune). In the world of the "text," because it is ruled by the law of "kinde" or nature, the grief of the two lovers cannot be transcended. As a result of the existential limitations of "carnal affection," as explained by Reason in *The Judgment of the King of Bohemia* (lines 1709–15), their sorrow proves irremediable.

With this in mind, we may now move to that section of Chaucer's work where the influence of Machaut's earlier poem is strongest. Chaucer's narrator falls asleep after reading in his book, and, dreaming, meets a man who has suffered a great loss. Just as Machaut's knight insists that the lady confess her troubles to him so that he may find their remedy, so the dreamer examines the Man in Black's sorrow in an attempt to help him overcome it. Chaucer's alterations in the pattern he borrowed from Machaut are notable, for the dialogue between the two characters in the dream, unlike Machaut's debate, focuses more directly from the very beginning on the healing power of reminiscence. In Machaut, as we have noted, the debate itself concerns what proves ultimately an empty question that, at John's court, is turned toward the important issue underlying it: the reconciliation of emotional idealism with the practical necessity of living in the world. Furthermore, in Machaut's poem the narrator is first a witness to the debate and then a guide for the disputants.

Chaucer, however, makes the dreamer an interlocutor, the other half of the debating pair. We can see this change as a result of Chaucer's broadening the role of the narrator he found in his source, where the narrator guides the turbulent expression of noble emotions only as far as his social position will permit, turning over the role of comforter to the more experienced and better qualified John. Chaucer's use of the dream-vision form as a setting for the dialogue means not only that the narrator's subjectivity never needs to be displaced but also that the social hierarchies of the waking world may be temporarily abandoned. The result is a dialogue that, making use of the conventional expressions of emotional idealism gleaned in a large measure from Machaut, probes that love experience more directly, less abstractly. The differences between the two works in this regard, however, do not derive from Chaucer's greater artistry so much as from the different rhetorical purposes the two poems were evidently designed to fulfill. Machaut's poem is both a demonstration of the poet's ability (hence his challenge for us to read it through the *Romance of the Rose*) and an extended compliment for the King of Bohemia. The *Book of the Duchess*, on the contrary, is an occasional piece which is intended as a consolation, much as Machaut's *Story of the Lovers' Fountain* (in which the narrator, appropriately enough, resembles Chaucer's more precisely). One way of looking at the relationship between *The Judgment of the King of Bohemia* and the *Book of the Duchess* would be, in fact, to maintain that Chaucer, in a large measure, has rewritten the debate of that earlier poem in the rhetorical form of *Story of the Lovers' Fountain*.

Much more so than any of its sources, however, Chaucer's poem is an examination of the love experience as this is embodied in the literary tradition of *dits amoreux*:

> In the *Book of the Duchess* the narrator's inconsolable melancholy exemplifies the dream's inability, despite its traditional wisdom, to rise to the heights of emotional idealism from which impermanence and mortality can be overcome. The dream itself climaxes not in any explanation of the rewards of faithful service by a comforting Venus, but rather in the plain words that clearly circumscribe the power of such visions. For this ending we have been prepared by the example of Alcyone. In a world that knows only natural love, she can find no solace for death. Ceyx' revelation of his own demise prompts her as well, and for this sorrow there is no metamorphosis as remedy.
>
> (Palmer 1980, 392–93)

Pelen (1976) similarly emphasizes that the *Book of the Duchess*, unlike *The Judgment of the King of Bohemia*, does not use the dialogue as the reason for the disputants to seek out a Court of Love, there to have their disagreement settled in an atmosphere that expresses the healing powers of love. But Chaucer's examination of the content and form of traditional poetry is, as was noted, also traditional, an element in the genre of the *dit amoreus* that can be traced at least as far as the interrogation of love in the second part of the *Romance of the Rose*. Like Machaut, in fact, Chaucer uses the narrator figure to express his exploration of the emotional idealism of that tradition, for he, too, is a poet writing and written by love poetry.

## Editorial Policy for This Text and Translation

Machaut's *Jugement dou Roy de Behaingne* is preserved in the following manuscripts, which are here preceded by the *sigla* assigned to them by Hoepffner and by which they are generally known:

### *Bibliothèque Nationale*

A: (14th century) BN 1584 Fond Français
B: (14th century) BN 1585 Fond Français
C: (15th century) BN 1586 Fond Français

D: (15th century) BN 1587 Fond Français
E: (14th century) BN 9221 Fond Français
F: (14th century) BN 22545 Fond Français
G: (14th century) BN 22546 Fond Français
M: (15th century) BN 843 Fond Français
P: (15th century) BN 2166 Fond Français
R: (15th century) BN 2230 Fond Français

K: (14th century) Berne 218
J: (14th century) Paris, Bibliothèque de L'Arsenal 5203
V or Vg: (15th century) in the Vogüé family collection
Of these MSS, only P and R are not more or less complete collections of Machaut's various works. In those two MSS the *Jugement dou Roy de Behaingne* is found within a heterogeneous collection of other works, attesting to its individual popularity.

In his edition of the narrative poems, Hoepffner maintains that a complete classification of the MSS must await modern and authoritative editing of all the works, a project which still has not yet reached completion. Hoepffner does construct a stemma to describe the filiation of the MSS based on his own work (which excludes both the *Voir Dit* and *La Prise d'Alexandrie* and which does not take direct account of MS Vg). A consideration of that stemma will provide a useful introduction to the problems faced by any editor in his attempts to construct an authoritative text of the various poems.

Only A and F contain the prologue, the four *ballades* of which are also found in E and H (BN 881 Fond Français, a partial collection of the *ballades* without musical text). These two MSS (and also G, which is a companion volume to F) must therefore be considered as containing the fullest collection of the works, since these likewise have all the other narrative and lyrical works found in the other cyclical MSS. Furthermore, A and FG usually give superior readings, though they are in no sense free from occasional scribal errors. Although it does not contain the prologue, M is closely related to A and FG. Hoepffner thus classifies these four MSS as an initial group which he, with good reason, considers to be closely related to Machaut's original MS O. And he also suggests, once again with good reason, that any edition of the poetry should be based on this group in some way.

A second family is formed by BDEKJ and a third by C and P (R and H are related at some remove to the antecedent of K). The divergences between the MSS of these two families and A and FG, as Hoepffner maintains, cannot be explained by the ordinary processes of textual transmission and scribal redaction, but rather by the fact, which can be inferred from Machaut's discussion of his poetry in the *Voir Dit*, that O, the poet's own exemplar, was naturally constituted little by little and often revised by the poet's own hand. These two second families, then, would have as their ultimate exemplar two different and earlier stages of O. With this in mind, Hoepffner decided to base his edition on A and FG (actually FG served as his copy text, at least for *Le Jugement dou Roy de Behaingne*). Where these MSS fail to provide adequate readings, Hoepffner maintained that the principle of common error should be invoked to yield the best reading:

> Agreement between AFG and BD guarantees a good reading; in the case of disagreement, A + BD should be in general preferred to FG, FG and BD to A, AFG to BD. (Hoepffner, *Oeuvres*, I, li.)

But the principle of common error, based on a stemma that takes as its assumption an original MS, is clearly inadequate here as a criterion of judgment. For that original MS, as Hoepffner's own research well establishes, was hardly stable, existing as it did in a number of versions as Machaut's career progressed. The principle of common error, however, assumes that variations from the original MS are in fact errors; as an editorial methodology it furnishes no criteria for distinguishing between true errors and the author's own revisions. This means that Hoepffner's editorial practice must be altered somewhat in order to produce a text that reflects the realities of Machaut's own artistic practice.

Therefore I have adopted A as the basis for the present edition. As we have seen, this MS bears a cachet (the inscription over the index) which seems to testify to Machaut's personal role in its production, for references to the author's wishes about the ordering of the text could only be the result of the author's intervention, given the medieval scribe's attitudes toward textual integrity in the modern sense. Because Machaut probably oversaw the production of this MS, I have adopted a conservative editorial policy, following the readings of A whenever they give reasonable sense and ignoring the principle of common error. As I see it, the editor's judgment in this situation must be limited to distinguishing between errors and variant readings (since both these categories can be determined by comparison with the other MSS). I have corrected A's readings only in those instances where, for various reasons, Machaut's intervention in the text could be reasonably ruled out. Whenever I determined A to be in error, I have substituted the reading of FG, if this seemed better, only very rarely having recourse to the other MSS. I have listed the variant readings of FG and the other MSS whenever these throw light on Machaut's revisions or illustrate a divergence from the copy text. The result is a text which only in minor ways differs from Hoepffner's, however, since A and FG present versions of the poem which are very much the same. Furthermore, I have followed Hoepffner in one way that a consideration of Machaut's practice and the double authority of A and FG both militate against: the inclusion in the printed text of four passages canceled from the latest versions of the poem (lines 980–83; 1000–47; 1816–19; and 1861–84). Hoepffner offers no justification for their inclusion, and one is certainly needed since, although they obviously belong to the "original" version of the poem, they are not a part of its final redaction. Scholarly discussion of *Le Jugement dou Roy de Behaingne*, however, is based on the numbering system of Hoepffner's edition. For this reason I have included the canceled passages as part of the text.

Any edition of a medieval text short of a completely diplomatic one naturally involves further decisions as to form. I have sometimes followed A in the division of the poem into sections (indicated by capital letters and spacing in the MS) when these seemed genuine rhetorical units; otherwise I have made my own divisions. Aside from modern treatments of *i* and *u* (which appear as *i/j* and *u/v* according to standard practice), I have retained the spelling irregularities of the MS except in one regard; I have substituted for *ay* for MS *ai* in verb forms such as *parlay*, etc., since this is the regular form in FG. MS numerals are represented in numeral form. I have punctuated the text with a view toward making it as readable as possible.

The job of a translator always calls for compromises of one kind or another, since the semantic complex and syntactic structures of the source language can never be converted into those of the target language with complete faithfulness. The translator of a Machaut narrative poem is immediately faced with a related problem: in English there is no stylistic register that corresponds to the love discourse that structures Machaut's verse. The syntax of late Old French, however, is very similar to that of Modern English. These two facts mean that the translator of Machaut can produce syntactic forms that are very much like those of the original (though the reader will notice that sometimes the word order of the poem must be abandoned in order to produce readable English prose); but he can discover semantic equivalents only for individual words or expressions, not for the complex paradigmatic relationships and semantic fields in the original discourse. The result is an English text that resembles the original closely in form and content but inevitably fails to reproduce its full meaning.

# Acknowledgments

This book would never have been conceived had Alan Gaylord and Charles T. Wood not fostered an undergraduate's interest in late medieval literature. And it could never have been written without the expert instruction in Old French that he received at the hands of V.E. Watts and Peter Haidu.

To Laila Gross and, especially, James Wilhelm a more immediate and substantial debt is owed. Whatever virtues the translation possesses are in large measure the result of their painstaking criticisms, though of course they are not responsible for any remaining inadequacies.

Many thanks are also owed to Georgia State University, particularly Dean Clyde Faulkner, for making available the released time necessary for the completion of the task. The dedication suggests a larger debt that can only be acknowledged, never repaid.

# Select Bibliography

## I. Editions of Guillaume de Machaut's Poetry

Chichmaref, V. *Guillaume de Machaut: Poésies lyriques.* 2 vols. Paris: Champion, 1909. Reliable edition of Machaut's large corpus of lyric poetry. Introduction contains some useful discussion of Machaut's life and the MS tradition but also contains a number of errors and must be used with caution.

Hoepffner, Ernest. *Oeuvres de Guillaume de Machaut.* Société des Anciens Textes Français. 3 vols. Paris: Firmin-Didot, 1908–21. A most impressive but unfortunately never completed edition of the narrative poetry. The only modern edition of *Jugement dou Roy de Behaingne.* Includes *Prologue, Jugement dou Roy de Behaingne, Jugement dou Roy de Navarre, Le Lay de Plour* (Volume I); *Remede de Fortune, Le Dit dou Lyon, Le Dit de l'Alerion* (Volume II); and *Le Confort d'Ami, La Fonteinne Amoureuse* (Volume III). Valuable introductory material. Useful short biography of the poet.

Mas Latrie, L. de. *La Prise d'Alexandrie ou Chronique du roi Pierre Ier.* Genève: Flick, 1877.

Paris, Paulin. *Le Livre du Voir-Dit de Guillaume de Machaut.* Paris: Société des Bibliophiles François, 1875. Inadequate edition according to modern standards. Numerous passages from MSS deleted without comment. A new edition of this poem is currently being compiled by Paul Imbs.

Wilkens, Nigel. *La Louange des Dames.* Edinburgh: Scottish Academic Press, 1972. Useful edition of the lyric poetry.

Wimsatt, James I. *The Marguerite Poetry of Guillaume de Machaut.* Chapel Hill: University of North Carolina, 1970. Excellent edition of some minor poems. Helpful commentary and discussion.

# II. Criticism and Study Guides

Amon, Nicole. "Le Vert: Guillaume de Machaut, poète de l'affirmation et de la joie." *Revue du Pacifique*, 2 (1976), 3–11. Discusses color symbolism in the *Voir Dit*.

Beer, Jeanette M.A. "The Ambiguity of Guillaume de Machaut." *Parergon*, 27 (1980), 27–31.

Bossuat, Robert. *Le Moyen Age: Histoire de la littérature française*, I. Paris: Del Duca, 1931. Contains a well-written and brief discussion of Machaut in the context of fourteenth-century literature.

Brownlee, Kevin. "The Poetic *Oeuvre* of Guillaume de Machaut: The Identity of Discourse and the Discourse of Identity." In Cosman and Chandler, 219–33. Important discussion of Machaut's conception of himself as poet. Useful analysis of the *Prologue*.

————. "Transformations of the lyric 'Je': The Example of Guillaume de Machaut." *L'Esprit Créateur*, 18 (1978), 5–18. Interesting analysis of Machaut's career and the relationship between his lyric and narrative poetry.

Calin, William. "A Reading of Machaut's *Jugement dou Roy de Navarre*." *Modern Language Review*, 66 (1971), 294–97.

————. *A Poet at the Fountain: Essays on the Narrative Verse of Guillaume de Machaut*. Lexington: Kentucky, 1974. The only full-length critical treatment of Machaut's narrative poetry. Full of useful information and interesting interpretations, but from an ahistorical approach. Bibliography.

————. "The Poet at the Fountain: Machaut as Narrative Poet." In Cosman and Chandler, 177–87.

————. "Problèmes de technique narrative au moyen-âge: Le *Roman de la Rose* et Guillaume de Machaut." In *Mélanges de langue et littérature françaises du moyen-âge offerts à Pierre Jonin*. Paris: Champion, 1979, 125–38. Treats relationship of Machaut's narrative poetry to the *Romance of the Rose*.

Chailley, Jacques. "Du cheval de Guillaume de Machaut à Charles II de Navarre." *Romania*, 94 (1973), 251–57.

Cosman, Madeleine Pelner, and Bruce Chandler, edd. *Machaut's World: Science and Art in the Fourteenth Century*. Annals of the New York Academy of Sciences, 314. New York: Academy of Sciences, 1978.

Indispensable collection of useful and appreciative analyses of the various aspects of Machaut's career.

Ehrhart, Margaret J. "Guillaume de Machaut's *Jugement dou Roy de Navarre* and Medieval Treatments of the Virtues." *Annuale Mediaevale, 19* (1979), 46–67.

――――. "Guillaume de Machaut's *Jugement dou Roy de Navarre* and the Book of Ecclesiastes." *Neuphilologische Mitteilungen, 81* (1980), 318–25.

――――. "The 'Esprueve de Fines Amours' in Guillaume de Machaut's *Dit dou lyon* and Medieval Interpretations of Circe and Her Island." *Neophilologus, 64* (1980), 38–41.

Faral, Edmond. *Recherches sur les sources latines des contes et romans courtois du moyen âge.* Paris: Champion, 1913. Important discussion of the relationship between Latin literature and vernacular love poetry.

Gunn, Allan F. *The Mirror of Love: A Re-Interpretation of "The Romance of the Rose."* Lubbock: Texas Tech Press, 1952. Useful discussion of backgrounds of the love-vision genre.

Haidu, Peter. "Making it (New) in the Middle Ages: Towards a Problematics of Alterity." *Diacritics, 4* (1974), 2–11. Important discussion of poetic originality and the criteria for its analysis and judgment in medieval French poetry.

Hieatt, Constance. "*Une Autre Forme*: Guillaume de Machaut and the Dream Vision Form." *Chaucer Review, 14* (1979), 97–115.

Hoepffner, Ernest. "Anagramme und Rätselgedichte bei Guillaume de Machaut." *Zeitschrift für romanische Philologie, 30* (1906), 401–13. Discusses the anagrams which close a number of Machaut poems, including *The Judgment of the King of Bohemia.*

Johnson, L.W. "'Nouviaus dis amoureux plaisans': Variation as Innovation in Guillaume de Machaut." *Le Moyen Francais, 5* (1979), 11–28.

Jung, Marc-René. *Études sur le poème allégorique en France au moyen âge. Romanica Helvetica, 82.* Berne: Francke, 1971. Studies allegorical poetry of the High Middle Ages. Useful analysis of love-debate genre.

Kelly, Douglas J. *Medieval Imagination: Rhetoric and the Poetry of Courtly Love.* Madison: Wisconsin, 1978. A full chapter on Machaut's narrative poetry. Intriguing discussion of the narrative poems in relationship to the *Romance of the Rose.* Traces Boethian influence. Full bibliography.

Kittredge, George L. *Chaucer and His Poetry.* Cambridge: Harvard, 1915. Important early document in the scholarly dismissal of Machaut.

Klapp, O., ed. *Bibliographie der französischen Literatur-wissenschaft/Bibliographie d'histoire littéraire.*

Langlois, Ernest. *Origines et sources du "Roman de la rose."* Paris: Champion, 1890. Discusses sources of the *Romance of the Rose,* including the love-debate poems.

Lanoue, D.G. "History as Apocalypse: the Prologue of Machaut's *Jugement dou Roy de Navarre." Philological Quarterly,* 60 (1981), 1–12.

Machabey, Armand. *Guillaume de Machaut, 130?–1377: La Vie et l'oeuvre musicale.* 2 vols. Paris: Richard-Masse, 1955. The fullest biography of Machaut.

Manley Williams, Sarah Jane. "An Author's Role in Fourteenth-Century Book Production: Guillaume de Machaut's 'livre où je met toutes mes choses.'" *Romania,* 90 (1969), 433–54. This and the following article are concerned with Machaut's poetic career.

————. "Machaut's Self-Awareness as Author and Producer." In Cosman and Chandler, 189–97.

Oulmont, Charles. *Les Débats du clerc et du chevalier dans la littérature poétique du moyen-âge.* Paris: Champion, 1911. Somewhat unreliable edition of love-debate texts. Some discussion of the genre's background.

Palmer, R. Barton. "Vision and Experience in Machaut's *Fonteinne Amoureuse." Journal of the Rocky Mountain Medieval and Renaissance Association,* 2 (1981), 79–86.

Poirion, Daniel. *Le Moyen Age.* Littérature Francaise, 2. Paris: B. Arthaud, 1971. Contains an excellent general discussion of Machaut's career in the context of late medieval French poetry.

————. *Le Poète et le prince: l'évolution du lyrisme courtois de Guillaume de Machaut à Charles d'Orléans.* Paris: Presses Universitaires de France, 1965. Although Poirion's main concern is the lyric poetry, this study is invaluable for its treatment of Machaut's narrative works as well. Important discussion of social context. Useful bibliography.

————. "The Imaginary Universe of Guillaume de Machaut." In Cosman and Chandler, 199–206. Interesting discussion of the implied world of Machaut's poetry, stressing the Boethian influence.

Prioult, A. "Un Poète Voyageur: Guillaume de Machaut et la *Reise* de Jean L'Aveugle, roi de Bohème, en 1328–9." *Lettres Romanes*, 4 (1950), 3–29. Discusses Machaut's relationship with John of Bohemia.

Roy, Maurice. *Oeuvres Poètiques de Christine de Pisan*. Vol. II. Paris: Firmin-Didot, 1891. Contains an edition of her *Le Livre du dit de Poissy*.

Rychner, Jean. "La flèche et l'anneau (sur les dits narratifs)." *Revue des Sciences Humaines*, 183 (1981), 55–69. Relates the narrative poetry to the *Romance of the Rose*. Dismisses *The Judgment of the King of Bohemia* as didactic, having no concern with "the real."

Uitti, Karl D. "From *Clerc* to *Poète*: The Relevance of the *Romance of the Rose* to Machaut's World." In Cosman and Chandler, 209–16. Guillaume de Lorris and Jean de Meun established the vernacular poet as an author in the classical sense. Machaut continued in this tradition.

Walther, H. *Das Streitgedicht in der lateinischen Literatur des Mittelalters*. Quellen und Untersuchungen zur lateinischen Philologie des Mittelalters, 5. Part Two. München: C.H. Beck'sche, 1920. Discussion of debate genre.

# III. Comparative Studies of Chaucer and Machaut

Brewer, Derek S. "The Relationship of Chaucer to the English and European Traditions." In *Chaucer and Chaucerians: Critical Studies in Middle English Literature*. Tuscaloosa: Alabama, 1966, 1–38. A good general introduction to Chaucer's connections to medieval French poetry.

Clemen, Wolfgang. *Chaucer's Early Poetry*. London: Methuen and Co., 1963. Notable for its inaccurate and distorted appraisal of Machaut. Continues traditional view of Chaucer as "creative" and Machaut as "conventional."

Harrison, Benjamin S. "Medieval Rhetoric in the *Book of the Duchesse*." *Publications of the Modern Language Association*, 49 (1934), 428–42.

Kittredge, George L. "Chauceriana. I. *The Book of the Duchess* and Guillaume de Machaut." *Modern Philology*, 7 (1909–10), 465–71. In this and the following three articles Kittredge pinpointed the dependence of Chaucer on Machaut noted in general terms by earlier scholars such as Sandras and Ten Brink.

————. "Chauceriana. II. 'Make the metres of hem as thee leste.'" *Modern Philology,* 7 (1909–10), 471–74.

————. "Chaucer's *Troilus* and Guillaume de Machaut." *Modern Language Notes,* 30 (1915), 69.

————. "Guillaume de Machaut and *The Book of the Duchess.*" *Publications of the Modern Language Association,* 30 (1915), 1–24.

Lowes, John L. "Chaucer and the *Ovide Moralisé.*" *Publications of the Modern Language Association,* 33 (1918), 302–25.

Meech, Sanford Brown. "Chaucer and the *Ovide Moralisé*: A Further Study." *Publications of the Modern Language Association,* 46 (1931), 182–204.

Muscatine, Charles. *Chaucer and the French Tradition: A Study in Style and Meaning.* Berkeley: California, 1957. Argues for the appreciation of Chaucer's conventionalness, but depreciates the influence of Machaut.

Palmer, R. Barton. "*The Book of the Duchess* and *Fonteinne Amoureuse*: Chaucer and Machaut Reconsidered." *Canadian Review of Comparative Literature,* 7 (1980), 380–93. Discusses Chaucer's exploration of the meaning of the love experience that is the subject of Machaut's poetry, especially *Fonteinne Amoureuse.*

Pelen, Marc M. "Machaut's Court of Love Narratives and Chaucer's *Book of the Duchess.*" *Chaucer Review,* 11 (1976), 128–55. Suggests that the Court of Love is a modernization of the "heavenly Neo-Platonic adjudicating epithalamic councils of Martianus Capella" and other late Latin poets. Chaucer alters its meaning as he found it in Machaut. Much useful detail and information.

Robbins, Rossell Hope. "Geoffroi Chaucier, poète français, Father of English Poetry." *Chaucer Review,* 13 (1978), 93–115.

Robertson, D.W., Jr. *A Preface to Chaucer: Studies in Medieval Perspectives.* Princeton: University Press, 1962. Important and still controversial study of the context of Chaucer's poetry.

Robinson, F.N., ed. *The Complete Works of Geoffrey Chaucer.* 2nd ed. Cambridge: Harvard, 1957.

Schilperoort, Johanna Catharina. *Guillaume de Machaut et Christine de Pisan (étude comparative).* The Hague: Mouton, 1936. General discussion of Machaut's influence on other poets, especially Pizan.

Severs, J. Burke. "The Sources of *The Book of the Duchess*." *Mediaeval Studies*, 25 (1963), 355–62.

Wimsatt, James I. "The Apotheosis of Blanche in *The Book of the Duchess*." *Journal of English and Germanic Philology*, 66 (1967), 26–44.

————. "Chaucer and French Poetry." In Derek Brewer, ed. *Geoffrey Chaucer*. Athens: Ohio University, 1975, 109–36. An important early document in the current re-evaluation of Machaut's poetry.

————. *Chaucer and the French Love Poets: The Literary Background of the Book of the Duchess*. University of North Carolina Studies in Comparative Literature, 43. Chapel Hill, North Carolina: University of North Carolina Press, 1968. A thorough study, including plot summaries, of the *dits amoreux* tradition. Full chart of sources of the *Book of the Duchess*.

————. "Guillaume de Machaut and Chaucer's *Troilus and Criseyde*." *Medium Aevum*, 45 (1976), 277–93. Rejects the views of both Muscatine and Kittredge that Chaucer "outgrew" his dependence on Machaut. Suggests that all of the important features of the *Troilus* find their analogues in Machaut's poetry.

————. "The Sources of Chaucer's 'Seys and Alcyone.'" *Medium Aevum*, 36 (1967), 231–41.

The Judgment of the King of Bohemia
Le Jugement dou Roy de Behaingne

Au temps pascour que toute riens s'esgaie,
Que la terre de mainte colour gaie
Se cointoie, dont pointure sans plaie
          Sous la mamelle
Fait Bonne Amour a mainte dame bele,                                    5
A maint amant et a mainte pucele,
Dont il ont puis mainte lie nouvelle
          Et maint esmay,
A ce dous temps, contre le mois de may,
Par un matin cointement m'acesmay,                                     10
Com cils qui trés parfaitement amay
          D'amour seüre.
Et li jours fu attemprez par mesure,
Biaus, clers, luisans, nès et purs, sans froidure.
La rousée par dessus la verdure                                       15
          Resplendissoit
Si clerement que tout m'esbloïssoit,
Quant mes regars celle part guenchissoit,
Pour le soleil qui dessus reluisoit.
          Et cil oisel,                                                20
Pour la douceur dou joli temps nouvel,
Si liement et de si grant revel
Chantoient tuit que j'alay a l'appel
          De leur dous chant.
Si en choisi en l'air un voletant                                      25
Qui dessus tous s'en aloit glatissant:
"Oci! Oci!" Et je le sievi tant*
          Qu'en un destour,
Sus un ruissel, près d'une bele tour
Ou il avoit maint arbre et mainte flour                                30
Souëf flairant, de diverse colour,
          S'ala sëoir.
Lors me laissay tout belement chëoir
Et me coïti si bien, a mon povoir,
Sous les arbres, qu'il ne me pot vëoir,                                35
          Pour escouter
Le trés dous son de son joli chanter.
Si me plut tant en oïr deliter
Son dous chanter, que jamais raconter
          Ne le porroie.                                               40

Mais tout einsi, com je me delitoie
En son trés dous chanter que j'escoutoie,
Je vi venir par une estroite voie,
          Pleinne d'erbette,
Une dame pensant, toute seulette                                       45
Fors d'un chiennet et d'une pucelette.


42. A jescoute

2

In the Easter season, when every creature takes heart,
When the earth with many joyful colors
Adorns herself, when Good Love without a wound
            Pierces
Beneath the breast of many a pretty lady,                    5
Of many lovers and many young girls,
And from this prick they have many new joys
            And also many cares,
At this sweet time, close to the month of May,
One morning I elegantly dressed,                             10
Like one who has loved most perfectly
            With a love secure.
And the day was balmy (just enough),
Pretty, clear, shiny, crisp and pure, without a chill.
The dew on the greenery                                      15
            Was shimmering
So clearly that everything blinded me,
When my look that way would turn,
Because of the sun which shone down from above.
            And the birds,                                   20
Because of the sweetness of the joyous new season,
So happily and with such grand celebration
All sang that I walked along to the call
            Of their sweet song.
Then among them I spied one in flight                        25
Who, above the others, was soaring as he cried:
"Oci !  Oci !"  And I followed him until
            In a solitary place
Above a stream, close to a beautiful tower,
Where there were many trees and many flowers                 30
Agreeably in bloom, of different colors,
            He perched.
Then I dropped quite pleasantly to the ground
And hid myself so well, as best I could,
Beneath the trees, that he could not see me,                 35
            In order to hear
The full sweet sound of his pleasant song.
And so it pleased me so much to have delight in hearing
His sweet singing, that I could never
            Describe it.                                     40


But all at once, as I delighted
In his very sweet singing, to which I was listening,
I saw approach by a narrow path,
            Full of short grass,
A lady deep in thought and all alone                         45
Save for a little dog and a serving girl.

Mais bien sambloit sa maniere simplette
       Pleinne d'anoy.
Et d'autre part, un petit long de moy,
Uns chevaliers de moult trés noble arroy          50
Tout le chemin venoit encontre soy
       Sans compaingnie;
Si me pensay qu'amis yert et amie.
Lors me boutay par dedens la fueillie          *[10r]*
Si embrunchiez qu'il ne me virent mie.*      55
       Mais quant amis,
En qui Nature assez de biens a mis,
Fu aprochiez de la dame de pris,
Com gracieus, sages, et bien apris
       La salua.               60
Et la dame que pensée argua,*
Sans riens respondre a li, le trespassa.
Et cils tantost arriere rappassa,
       Et si la prist
Par le giron, et doucement li dist:          65
"Trés douce dame, avez vous en despit
Le mien salut?" Et quant elle le vit,
       Si respondi
En souspirant, que plus n'i atendi:
"Certes, sire, pas ne vous entendi          70
Pour mon penser qui le me deffendi;
       Mais si j'ay fait
Riens ou il ait villonie ou meffait,
Vueilliez le moy pardonner, s'il vous plait."
Li chevaliers, sans faire plus de plait,      75
       Dist doucement:
"Dame, il n'affiert ci nul pardonement,
Car il n'i a meffait ne mautalent;
Mais je vous pri que vostre pensement
       Me vueilliez dire."         80
Et la dame parfondement sospire
Et dist: "Por Dieu, laissiez m'en pais, biau sire,
Car mestier n'ay que me faciez plus d'ire
       Ne de contraire
Que j'en reçoy." Et cils se prist a traire      85
Plus près de li, pour sa pensée attraire,
Et li a dit: "Trés douce debonnaire,
       Triste vous voy.
Mais je vos jur et promet par may foy,
S'a moy volez descouvrir vostre anoy,      90
Que je feray tout le pooir de moy
       De l'adrecier."
Et la dame l'en prist a mercïer,
Et dist: "Sire, nuls ne m'en puet aïdier,

55. AF embunchiez; BR embuschez--61. AFBE qui

But her innocent manner obviously appeared
                Full of distress.
And on the other side, a little distance from me,
A knight of very noble array                                    50
Came right toward her down the path
                Without company;
And so it seemed they might be lover and beloved.
Then I pushed myself inside the leaves,
So hidden I was that they could not see me at all.             55
                But when that lover,
To whom Nature had granted her considerable gifts,
Had approached that lady of worth,
Like a gracious gentleman, wise and well-mannered,
                He greeted her.                                 60
And the lady who was oppressed by thought,
Without responding to him, passed him by.
And he turned back at once,
                And then took her
By the robe, and softly said to her:                           65
"My sweet lady, have you scorn
For my greeting?"  And when she saw him,
                She answered
Sighing,  that she'd not attended to it:
"To be sure, sir, I heard you not at all                       70
Because my thoughts prevented it;
                But if I've done
Anything ignoble or impolite,
Please pardon me for it, if you would."
The knight, without more argument,                             75
                Said softly:
"Lady, no pardon here is needed,
For there has been no misdeed or wrong intention;
But I beg you please tell me
                Your thoughts."                                80
Then the lady deeply sighed
And said: "For the sake of God, leave me in peace, fair sir,
For I don't need you to increase the anxiety
                Or the frustration
That I receive from them."  At this he began to move           85
Closer to her, to draw out her thoughts,
And said to her: "Very sweet and noble one
                I see you're sad.
But I swear to you and promise by my faith
That, if you'd reveal your troubles to me,                     90
I would do everything in my power
                To put them right."
And the lady undertook to thank him for this
And said: "Sir, no one can help me in this,

Ne nuls fors Dieus ne porroit alegier                    95
        La grief dolour
Qui fait palir et teindre ma coulour,
Qui tient mon cuer en tristesse et en plour,
Et qui me met en si dure langour
        Qu'a dire voir                                    100
Nuls cuer qui soit n'en porroit plus avoir."
"Dame, et quels mauls vos fait si fort doloir?
Dites le moy; que je cuit recevoir
        Si trés grief peinne,
Si dolereuse, si dure, si greveinne,                      105
Si amere, que soiez bien certeinne,
Il n'est dame, ne creature humeinne,
        Ne n'iert jamais,
Qui tele peinne endurast onques mais."
"Certes, sire, je croy bien que tel fais                  110
Ne portez pas a vo cuer que je fais.
        Pour ce sarez
Ma pensée qu'a savoir desirez.
Mais tout avant, vos me prometterez
Que sans mentir la vostre me direz."                      115
        "Tenez, ma dame.
Je vous promet par may foy et par m'ame
Que le penser qui m'esprent et enflame
Et qui souvent mon cuer mort et entame
        Vous gehiray                                      120
De chief en chief, ne ja n'en mentiray."
"Certes, sire, et je le vous diray."
"Or dites donc; je vous escouteray
        Moult volentiers."


"Sire, il a bien .vij. ans ou .viij. entiers             125
Que mes cuers a esté sers et rentiers
A Bonne Amour, si qu'apris ses sentiers
        Ay trés m'enfance.
Car dès premiers que j'eus  sa congnoissance,
Cuer, corps, povoir, vie, avoir, et puissance            130
Et quanqu'il fu de moy, mis par plaisance
        En son servage.
Et elle me retint en son hommage
Et me donna de trés loial corage                         [10v]
A bel et bon, dous, gracieus, et sage,                    135
        Qui de valour,
De courtoisie et de parfaite honnour,
Et de plaisant maintient avoit la flour,
Et des trés bons estoit tout le millour.
        Et s'ot en li                                     140


126. A renties--131. A plaisence

6

Nor none save God could alleviate                                95
          The terrible grief
Which taints and pales my complexion,
Which holds fast my heart in sorrow and in tears,
Which leaves me in such hard languor
          That, to tell the truth,                              100
No heart that exists could ever have more."
"Lady, what misfortune makes your pain so great?
Tell it to me; for I think to have received
          A hurt so very painful
So sorrowful, so strong, so heavy,                             105
So bitter that, of this you may be sure,
There is no woman, no human being,
          And never was,
Who has ever endured this kind of pain."
"Surely, sir, I firmly believe that you                        110
Bear not the same burden in your heart that I do.
          Therefore you'll know
My thoughts as you have wished.
But, before all this, you will promise me
To tell me yours without any lies."                            115
          "Agreed, my lady.
I promise you by my faith and by my soul
That the thought which inflames and burns me
And which often eats at my heart and rends it
          I will confess to you                                120
Completely, and in nothing will I lie."
"So be it, sir, and now I'll tell you mine."
"Speak then, and I will listen to you
          Most willingly."

"Sir, altogether now it's seven years or eight                 125
That my heart's been serf and vassal
To Good Love, whose ways I have come to learn
          Since my childhood.
For when I encountered Love the first time
I gladly placed heart, body, strength, life,                   130
My goods and power, whatever there was of me,
          At her disposal.
As her vassal she retained me
And entrusted to me the loyal heart
Of one who was handsome and good, sweet, wise, and gracious,
          Who in valor,
In courtesy, in perfect honor,
In his pleasant demeanor was the very flower,
And of the very good was indeed the best.
          And he had                                           140

7

Gent corps faitis, cointe, apert, et joli,
Juene, gentil, de maniere garni,
Plein de tout ce qu'il faut a vray ami.
   Et d'estre amez
Par dessus tous estoit dignes clamez, 145
Car il estoit vrais, loiaus, et secrez,
Et en trestous fais amoureus discrez;*
   Et je l'amoie
Si loiaument que tout mon cuer mettoie
En li amer, n'autre entente n'avoie; 150
Qu'en li estoit m'esperence, ma joie,
   Et mon plaisir,
Mon cuer, m'amor, mon penser, mon desir.
De tous les biens pooit mes cuers joïr
Par li veoïr seulement et oïr. 155
   Tous mes confors
Estoit en li; c'estoit tous mes depors,
Tous mes solas, mes deduis, mes tresors.
C'estoit mes murs, mes chastiaus, mes ressors.
   Et il m'amoit; 160
Par dessus tout me servoit et cremoit;
Son cuer, s'amour, sa dame me clamoit.
Tous estoit miens; mes cuers bien le savoit;
   Ne riens desplaire
Ne li peüst qui a moy deüst plaire 165
De nos .ij. cuers estoit si juste paire
Qu'onques ne fu l'un a l'autre contraire;
   Einsois estoient
Tuit d'un acort; une pensée avoient.
De volenté, de desir se sambloient; 170
Un bien, un mal, une joie sentoient
   Conjointement,
N'onques ne fu entre eaus .ij. autrement;
Mais c'a esté toudis si loyaument
Qu'il n'ot onques un villain pensement 175
   En nos amours.
Lasse, dolente! Or est bien a rebours.
Car mes douceurs sont dolereus labours,
Et mes joies sont ameres dolours,
   Et mi penser, 180
En qui mes cuers se soloit deliter
Et doucement de tous maus conforter,
Sont et seront dolent, triste, et amer.
   En obscurté
Seront mi jour, plein de maleürté, 185
Et mi espoir sans nulle seürté,
Et ma douceur sera dure durté

147. AFMB et discrez--174. F toudis este

A noble body, elegant too, gracious, well-formed, and pleasing;
He was young, genteel, well-mannered,
Full of all things needed in a true lover.
                And to be loved
Above all others he was called worthy.                    145
For he was true, loyal, and circumspect,
And in what pertained to love discreet;
                And I loved him
So loyally that all of my heart I put
Into loving him, no other thought did I have;              150
So that in him was my hope, my joy,
                And my pleasure,
My heart, my love, my thoughts, and my desire.
In every kind of goodness my heart could rejoice
Only by seeing and hearing him.                            155
                All of my comfort
Lay in him; he was all that pleased me,
All my solace, my delight, my treasure.
He was my wall, my castle, my refuge.
                And he loved me;                           160
Above all else he served and venerated me;
He called me his heart, his love, his lady;
He was mine completely; my heart knew him well.
                Nor could anything
Displease him that should please me.                       165
Our true hearts were so true a pair
That never was one contrary to the other;
                Rather they were
Always in accord; one thought they shared.
In will and in desire they were the same;                  170
A single good, one evil, one joy they felt
                Together,
And never was it otherwise between those two;
But because everything always went so loyally
There never was an ignoble thought                         175
                In our loving.
Alas! What sorrow! Now the opposite is true.
For what was sweetness now is painful suffering,
What was joy is now bitter hurt,
                And my thoughts,                           180
In which my heart did once take delight
And sweetly found solace for every hurt,
Are painful, bitter, sad, and will so remain:
                In darkness
Will my days remain, filled with misadventure,             185
And my hope without any certainty,
And my sweetness will become a lasting hardness;

9

                    Car sans faillir
Teindre, trambler, muer, et tressaillir,
Pleindre, plourer, souspirer, et gemir,                          190
Et en paour de desespoir fremir
                    Me couvendra;
N'a mon las  cuer jamais bien ne vendra,
N'a nul confort n'a joie n'ateindra,*
Jusques atant que la mort me prendra,                            195
                    Qui a grant tort
Par devers moy, quant elle ne s'amort
A moy mordre de son dolereus mort,
Quant elle m'a dou tout tollu et mort
                    Mon dous amy                                 200
Que j'amoie de fin cuer et il my.
Mais après li, lasse! Dolente! Eimy!
Ne quier jamais vivre jour ne demi
                    En si grief dueil;
Eins vueil mourir dou mal dont je me dueil."                     205
Et je, qui fu boutez dedens le brueil,
Vi qu'a ce mot la dame au dous acueil
                    Chei com morte.
Mais cils qui fu de noble et gentil sorte
Souventes fois li deprie et enorte                               210
Moult doucement qu'elle se reconforte,
                    Mais riens ne vaut;
Car la dame que grief doleur assaut
Pour son ami sent .i. si dur assaut                              [11r]
Qu'en li vigour et alainne deffaut.                              215
                    Et quant il voit
Que la dame pas ne l'entent ne oit,
Tant fu dolens qu'estre plus ne pooit.
Mais nonpourquant tant fait que bien parçoit
                    Qu'elle est pasmée.                          220
Lors en sa main cueilli de la rousée
Sus l'erbe vert; si l'en a arrousée
En tous les lieus de sa face esplourée
                    Si doucement
Que la dame qui avoit longuement                                 225
Perdu vigour, scens, et entendement
Ouvri les yeus et prist parfondement
                    A souspirer,
En regretant celui qui desirer
Li fait la mort par loiaument amer.                              230
Mais cils qui ot le cuer franc sans amer
                    Dist: "Dame chiere,
Pour Dieu merci, reprenez vo maniere;
Vous vous tuez de faire tele chiere,


194. DEJKP nattendra

                Since inevitably
I must lose my color, tremble, change, and startle,
Moan, cry, sigh, and wail,                              190
And in my fear of despair
                Even shake;
Nor will any good ever come to my sad heart,
Nor any comfort, any joy ever touch it,
That is til death will take me,                        195
                Death who has greatly
Wronged me, in that she did not bring herself
To bite me with her mortal sting
When of everything she stripped me by killing
                My lover sweet,                        200
Whom I loved with a tender heart as he did me.
But after him, alas!  Sorrow!  What pain!
Not one day or even a half do I want to live
                In such terrible grief;
I would rather die from the sickness whose pain I feel."
And I, who lay pushed within the brush,
Saw that at this word the gracious lady
                Fell like one dead.
But he who was both gentle and kind
Many times did beg and exhort her                      210
Quite tenderly to comfort herself
                Though nothing availed;
For, assaulted by a grievous pain, the lady,
For her lover's sake, felt such a hard attack
That breath and strength both failed her.             215
                And when he saw
That the lady neither heard nor listened to him,
He was as worried as he could be.
But nonetheless he well perceived
                That she had fainted.                  220
Then in his hand he gathered some dew
From the green grass and sprinkled her with it
All over her tear-stained face
                So softly
That the lady who for so long a time                   225
Had lost her strength, reason, and understanding
Opened her eyes, and began deeply
                To sigh,
While mourning him who made her wish
Her death through faithful loving.                     230
But this man, whose heart was noble, without hardness
                Said: "Dear lady,
For God's sake, recover yourself;
You will kill yourself in going on like this,

Car je voy bien que moult comparez chiere                    235
        L'amour de li.
Si n'aiez pas le cuer einsi failli,
Car ce n'est pas preus, ne honneur aussi,"
"Vous dites voir, sire: mais trop mar vi
        L'eure et le jour                                    240
Qu'onques amay de si parfaite amour,
Car je n'en puis eschaper par nul tour:
Eins y congnois ma mort sans nul retour."
        "Dame, or oiez
Ce que diray, et a mal ne l'aiez.                            245
N'est merveille se vous vous esmaiez,*
Car bien est drois que dolente soiez.
        Mais vraiement
On trouveroit plus tost aligement
En vostre mal qu'en mien." "Sire, et comment?              250
Dites le moy, et de vo sairement
        Vous aquitez."
"Moult voulentiers, mais que vous m'escoutez,
Et que vo cuer de tristece gettez,
Par quoy toute vostre entente metez                         255
        A moy oïr."
"Certes, sire, po me puis resjoïr.
Mais j'en feray mon pooir, sans mentir."
"Dont vous diray quels maus j'ay a sentir,
        Sans plus attendre."                                260


"Dame, trés dont que je me sos entendre,
Et que mes cuers pot sentir et comprendre*
Que c'est amer, je ne finay de tendre
        A estre amez;
Si que lonc temps, por estre amis clamez,                   265
Eins que mes cuers fust assis ne donnez
N'a dame nulle ottroiez n'assenez,
        A Bonne Amour
Par maintes fois fis devote clamour
Qu'elle mon cuer asseïst a l'onnour                         270
De celle en qui il feroit son sejour,
        Et que ce fust
Si que loange et gloire en receüst
Et que, se ja mes cuers faire peüst
Chose de quoy souvenir li deüst                             275
        Ou desservir
Nul guerredon de dame par servir,
Qu'en aucun temps li deingnast souvenir
De moy qui vueil estre siens, sans partir,
        Toute ma vie.                                        280


246. CBDEKJR Nest pas meru--262. FMBDK ne comprendre

12

Since I see well you pay most dearly                        235
        For your love for him.
Yet let your heart not break so,
For in that lies neither advantage nor honor."
"You tell the truth, sir; for it was in adversity that I saw
        The hour and the day                               240
When I ever loved with such a perfect love,
Because in no way can I escape from it.
Instead, unflinchingly, I'll face my death."
        "Lady, now hear
What I will say, and please don't take it ill.             245
It is no wonder that you are distraught,
For certainly it's right you should be saddened.
        But truly
One could much sooner find relief
From your troubles that from mine." "Sir, how so?          250
Tell me this, and from your agreement
        You'll be released."
"Willingly, but listen to me
And remove your heart from sadness,
So that you can give all your attention                    255
        To listening to me."
"Surely, sir, I can rejoice but little.
Yet, I do not lie, I'll do my best."
"Then I'll tell you what pains I have to feel
        Without delaying further."                          260


"Lady, as soon as I did know myself,
And when my heart could feel and understand
What loving is, from that time I've never stopped striving
        To be loved;
Thus for a long time, in order to be called a lover,       265
Before my heart was fixed on or given,
Or granted, or even inclined to one lady,
        To Good Love
At many times I made devout request
That she'd place my heart to the honor                     270
Of her in whom it would find a home,
        And that this would be
In such a way that for it praise and glory would be hers
And that, if my heart could ever accomplish
Anything to make her remember it                           275
        Or earn merit
Or reward from the lady through serving her,
That at some time Love might deign to remember
Me, the man who would be her vassal, never to leave
        For all my life.                                    280

13

Tant qu'il avint qu'en une compaingnie
Ou il avoit mainte dame jolie,
Juene, gentil, joieuse, et envoisie,
      Vins par Fortune,
Qui de mentir a tous est trop commune,          285
Si en choisi entre les autres l'une
Qui, tout aussi com li solaus la lune
      Veint de clarté,*
Avoit elle les autres seurmonté
De pris, d'onneur, de grace, et de biauté,       290
Et tant estoit humble et simple, a mon gré,
      Car, a voir dire,
On ne porroit en tout le monde eslire
Sa pareille, ne tous li mons souffire          [11v]
Ne porroit pas por sa biauté descrire       295
      Parfaitement.
Car je la vi dancier si cointement
Et puis chanter si trés joliement,
Rire et jouer si gracieusement
      Qu'onques encor              300
Ne fu veüs plus gracieus tresor.*
Car si cheveus ressambloient fil d'or
Et n'estoient ne trop blont ne trop sor.*
      Son front estoit
Blanc et poli, ne fronce n'i avoit,           305
Sans vice nul compassé si a droit
Que trop large n'estoit, ne trop estroit;
      Et si sorcil,
Qui estoient de taille trés gentil,
Dessus le blanc sambloient .i. noir fil,      310
Dont il fussent prisié entre cent mil.
      Mais si .ij. oueil,
Qui de mon cuer vorrent passer le sueil
Par leur rigour et par leur bel accueil,
Pour moy donner le mal dont je me dueil,   315
      Furent riant,
Nom pas moult vair, por estre plus poingnant
Et plus agu, dous, humble, et attraiant,
Tous pleins de las pour loier .i. amant
      En amour pure;            320
Et s'estoient clungnetant par mesure,
Fendus a point, sans trop grant ouverture,
Tout acquerant par leur douce pointure;
      N'a l'entrouvrir
Ne se peüst nuls homs qui soit couvrir      325
Qu'en mi le cuer ne l'alassent ferir,
S'il leur pleüst, et pour euls retenir.

288. ABD la clarte--301. All other MSS veu--303. A blonc
307. FMB larges--323. A poiture

Until at last it happened that among a group
Where there were many pretty ladies,
Young, gentle, happy, and amusing,
      I chanced by Fortune
(Whose habit it is to lie to all)              285
And from the others I picked out one
Who, just as the sun surpasses the moon
      In brightness,
Had conquered all the others
In esteem, in honor, in grace, and beauty,      290
And was so serene and straightforward, to my liking,
      That to tell the truth
No one could find in all the world
Her equal, nor could the whole world itself suffice
To describe her beauty                    295
      Perfectly.
For I saw her dance so graciously,
And sing with such great joy,
Laugh and play so graciously
      That never yet                  300
Was ever seen a more elegant treasure.
For her hair resembled threads of gold
And was neither too light nor too dark.
      Her forehead was
White and smooth, no wrinkle there,      305
Without a flaw, of such correct proportion,
Since it was not too small and not too long.
      And her brows,
Which had a very noble shape,
Below that whiteness resembled black threads      310
And they were prized above a hundred thousand.
      But her two eyes,
Which wanted to pass the threshold of my heart
By their strength and by their fair welcome,
To endow me with the pain that grieves me so,      315
      Were smiling,
Not really very gray, so that they were more piercing,
And more striking, sweet, sober, and alluring,
All full of traps to snare a lover
      In pure love;                320
And they were half-shut,
Just wide enough, without too great an opening,
Conquering all by their sweet piercing;
      Nor in their opening
Could any man alive guard himself      325
So that they did not strike through his heart,
If it pleased them, to take him for their own.

```
                Mais leurs regars,
Merci donnant par samblant, aus musars
N'estoit mie folettement espars;                          330
Car quant lancier voloit .i. de ses dars,
           Si sagement
Le savoit faire et si soutivement
Que nuls savoir nel peüst bonnement,
Fors cils seur qui il chëoit proprement.                  335
           Net, odorant,
Lonc et traitif, de taille bien sëant
Avoit le nés au viaire afferant;
Car il n'estoit trop petit, ne trop grant.
           Mais sa bouchette,                             340
Petite a droit, vermillette, grossette,
Toudis riant, savoreuse, doucette,
Me fait languir, quant mes cuers la regrette.
           Car qui l'oïst
Parler a point, et rire la vëist,                         345
Et les douceurs par saveur recueillist,
Il la prisast seur toutes et dëist;
           Que .ij. fossettes
En sousriant faisoient ses joettes
Qui estoient blanches et vermillettes                     350
Pour embelir, et un petit grassettes.
           Et encor plus:
Les dens avoit blans, sarrez, et menus,
Et ses mentons estoit un po fendus,
Votis dessous et rondez par dessus.                       355
           Mais a merveille
Fu sa coulour, des autres nompareille,
Car elle fu vive, fresche, et vermeille,
Plus que la rose en may, eins qu'on la cueille;
           Et, a briés mos,                               360
Blanche com noif, polie, de biau gros
Fu sa gorge, n'i ot fronce ne os;
Et s'ot biau col dont je la pris et los.
           Aussi est drois
Que je parle de ses bras lons et drois,                   365
Qui estoient bien fais en tous endrois;
Car elle avoit blanches mains et lons dois.
           A mon devis
Avoit le sein blanc, dur, et haut assis,
Pongnant, rondet, et si estoit petis,                     370
Selonc le corps, gracieus, et faitis.
           Sans nul mestret
Avoit le corps par mesure pourtret,
Gent, joint, joli, juene, gentil, grasset,          [12r]
```

337. CEKJP traitiz--367. MCEKJ Et si

```
              But their look,
Which seemed to grant mercy, to dawdlers
Was not at all unwisely parceled out,                    330
For when she wished to launch from her eyes a dart,
            So craftily
She knew how to do it and so subtly
That no one could ever  truly know
Except him upon whom it properly fell.                   335
            Pretty, dainty,
Long and straight, of a size well suited to her
Was her nose, its shape agreeable;
For it was neither too big nor too small;
              But her little mouth                       340
Was just small enough, rose-colored, a bit rounded,
Always smiling, delicious, and sweet;
It makes me languish when my heart mourns her.
            For whoever heard her
Speak so well, and saw her laugh,                        345
And received with pleasure the sweetness
Would value her above all others, and say as much;
            For two dimples
In smiling her cheeks would make,
Which were white and rosy,                               350
To increase their beauty, and they were a bit rounded.
            And even more:
Her teeth were white, small, and even,
And her chin was a little wide,
Arched below and rounded all above.                      355
            Wondrous indeed
Was her complexion, unlike all others,
For it was vibrant, fresh, and rosy,
More so than any rose in May before it's picked;
            And, in a few words,                         360
White as snow, smooth, pleasantly plump
Was her throat, and without any wrinkle or bone;
Her neck was beautiful, which I prize and praise.
            It's also fitting
That I speak of her arms, long and straight,            365
Which were in every way well-fashioned;
But her hands were white and her fingers long.
            As far as I could tell
Her bosom was white, firm, and high-seated,
Her breasts pointed, round, and small enough,           370
Suiting her body, gracious and agreeable.
            Without a flaw
Her body was rightly formed,
Noble, well-shaped, pretty, young, genteel, plump
```

```
Lonc, droit, faitis, cointe, apert, et graillet.          375
          Trés bien tailliez
Hanches, cuisses, jambes ot, et les piez,
Votis, grossez, bien et bel enjointiez,
Par maistrise mignotement chauciez.
          Dou remenant                                     380
Que pas ne vi, dame, vous di je tant
Qu'a nature tout estoit respondant,
Bien fassonné et de taille excellent.
          Et ce seurplus,
Dont je ne vueil maintenant dire plus,                     385
Devoit estre sans comparer tenus
A plus trés dous et a plus biaus que nuls.
          Delié cuirien
Blanc et souëf avoit, sus toute rien
Resplendissant, si qu'on si mirast bien;                   390
Vice, tache n'i avoit fors que bien
          Douce et serrée
Avoit la char, tendrette de rousée,
Mais de maniere humble et asseurée
Et de trés biau maintien estoit parée.                     395
          Et vraiement,
Tant fu belle, que je croy fermement,
Se Nature, qui tout fait soutilment,
En voloit faire une aussi proprement,
          Qu'elle y faurroit,                               400
Et que jamais assener n'i saroit,
Se l'exemple de ceste ci n'avoit,
Qui de biauté toutes autres passoit.
          Et se vous di
Qu'onques encor en ma vie ne vi                            405
Corps de dame si trés bien assevi.
Mais elle avoit xiiij. ans et demi
          Ou environ.
Si que, dame, quant je vi sa fasson,
Qui tant estoit bele sans meffaçon,                        410
Dedens mon cuer la douce impression
          De sa figure
Fu telement empreinte qu'elle y dure,
Ne onques puis n'en parti, dont j'endure
Meinte doleur et meinte durté dure.                        415
          Et sans doutance,
Eins que partis fusse de sa presence,
Dedens mon cuer se ficha si Plaisence,
En remirant sa douce contenance,
          Que sachiez bien,                                 420
Se j'eüsse l'avoir Othevien,*
```

Long, straight, pleasing, cute, agreeable, and svelte.      375
          Very well shaped
Were the hips, thighs, legs, and the feet were
Arched, plump, prettily and well put together,
Cunningly shod with delightful shoes.
          Of the rest                                        380
Which I did not see, lady, I'll tell you this,
That all answered Nature's demands;
Well-fashioned and of excellent shape it was.
          And what remains,
Of which right now I wish to say no more,                   385
Must be considered beyond compare,
Much more sweet and more beautiful than any.
          Her delicate skin
Was white and soft, more than all else
It shone, so that one marvelled at it;                       390
Flaw or fault was there none, only goodness.
          Sweet and firm
Was her flesh, young with moisture,
But she was endowed with a manner humble
And assured--she had a pleasing way about her.              395
          And to tell the truth
She was so beautiful (I hold this most firmly)
That, if Nature, who makes all things craftily,
Wished to make another just like her,
          She would fail.                                    400
And never would she know how to do it
If she did not have this one as a model,
Who surpasses all others in beauty.
          And so I tell you
That never have I seen in all my life                        405
A woman's body so very well formed.
And she was aged fourteen and a half
          Or thereabouts.
So, lady, when I beheld her appearance,
Which was so beautiful, without any flaw,                    410
Within my heart the sweet impression
          Of her image
Was so imprinted that still it endures there,
Nor ever since has parted from me, and so I suffer
Many pains and many enduring troubles.                       415
          And beyond all doubt,
As soon as I left her presence,
Pleasure so fixed itself within my heart
In marvelling at her sweet countenance,
          That you may be sure                                420
That, if I had Octavian's riches,

Et sceüsse le scens de Galien,
Et avec ce tuit li bien fussent mien,
                    Je tout eüsse
Guerpi par si, que veoir la peüsse                      425
A mon voloir, ou que faire sceüsse
Chose a son vueil, dont plaire li deüsse.
                    Mais Fine Amour,
Qui vit que pris estoie par le tour
De Plaisence, qui m'ot mis en sa tour,                  430
En remirant son gracieus atour,
                    Sans menacier
Un dous regart riant me fist lancier
Par mi le cuer, et moy si enlacier,
Qu'il me sousmist en son trés dous dangier,            435
                    Sans repentir.
Si me plut tant cils dangiers a sentir,
Quant cils regars se deingnoit assentir
A descendre sus moy que, sans mentir,
                    Je ne savoie                        440
Qu'il m'avenoit, ne quele part j'estoie,
Car scens, vigour, et maniere perdoie;
Si durement par ses yeus me sentoie
                    Enamourez.
Adont desirs d'estre de li amez                         445
En mon cuer fu si trés fort enflamez
Que puis m'en suis cent fois chetis clamez
                    En souspirant;
Car tel doleur sentoie en desirant
Que ma vigour en aloit empirant                        450
Et meint penser avoie, en remirant
                    Son dous viaire;
Car volentiers li alasse retraire                       [12v]
Comment de cuer l'amoie, sans retraire.
Mais la paour d'escondire ce faire                      455
                    Me deffendoit;
Et d'autre part Bel Acueil m'appelloit;
Son Dous Regart riant m'asseüroit,
Et Dous Espoirs doucement ce disoit
                    En loiauté,                         460
Et m'affermoit qu'onques si grant biauté
Ne pot estre, qu'il n'i eüst pité.
Si m'ont cil troi tant dit et enorté
                    Que toutevoie
Je m'acorday que m'amour li diroie.                     465
Helas!   Einsi   tous seuls me debatoie.
Mais quant mes maus retraire li cuidoie,
                    Si paoureus,


437. ECDKJ dangier--439. All other MSS seur

20

And knew all of Galen's science,
And, in addition, possessed all goods,
          All of it I would
Throw over, if only I could see her                      425
As I wish, or could accomplish anything
That she'd like, something that would please her.
          But Noble Love,
Who saw that I was captured by the trick
Of Pleasure, who'd locked me in her tower,                430
As I was marvelling at her gracious presence,
          Without threatening
She threw a sweet and laughing look
Straight through my heart, to trap me thus,
So that it made me submit to her very sweet domination   435
          Without repenting of it.
I was so pleased to feel this domination
When her look would deign
To fall upon me that (I do not lie)
          I didn't know                                  440
What happened to me or where I was,
Since senses, strength, and bearing I lost;
So forcefully I felt myself through her eyes
          Enamored
That the desire to be loved by her                       445
Was so fervently ignited in my heart
That then I called myself a miserable captive one hundred times
          While sighing;
For I felt such misery in my desiring
That continually my strength was failing me,             450
And my thoughts were all confused, while I contemplated
          Her sweet appearance.
But willingly I'd have gone to tell her
How with my heart I loved her, without retreating.
Yet the fear of being shamed by doing this               455
          Prevented me;
And on the other side Fair Welcome beckoned me;
His Sweet Look in smiling assured me,
And Sweet Hope spoke softly to me
          In loyalty,                                    460
And affirmed to me that such a great beauty
Could never exist, had pity not been with it.
Thus these three spoke so much and exhorted me so much
          That right away
I planned to tell her of my love.                        465
Alas! In this way all alone I argued with myself.
But when I thought to rehearse my pains to her,
          So fearful

Si veins, si mas, si las, si engoisseus,
Si desconfis, si tramblans, si honteus                          470
Estoit mes cuers et dou mal amoureus
          Si fort espris
Qu'en li n'avoit scens, maniere, n'avis,
Einsois estoit com transis et ravis,
Quant bien vëoir povoie vis a vis                               475
          Sa biauté pure.
Lors estoit mors d'amoureuse morsure
Mes cuers et poins de joieuse pointure
Et repeüs de douce nourreture
          Par Dous Penser,                                      480
Qui ma doleur faisoit toute cesser
Et garison me faisoit esperer.
Einsi souvent avoie pour amer
          Joie et tourment.
Si demouray en ce point longuement,                            485
Une heure liez et l'autre heure dolent,
Qu'onques n'osay requerre aligement
          De ma dolour.
Mais nompourquant grant destresse d'amour,
Ardant desir, la crueuse langour,                              490
Ou j'avoie demouré par maint jour,
          Son bel acueil,
Esperence de terminer mon dueil,
Sa grant biauté, si dous riant vair oueil,
Et ce qu'en li n'avoit goute d'orgueil,                        495
          Le hardement
De requerre merci couardement
Me donnerent; si li dis humblement,
Moult tresmuez et paoureusement:
          'Ma chiere dame,                                      500
Vostre biauté mon cuer art et enflame,
Si que seur tout vous aim, sans penser blame,
De cuer, de corps, de vray desir, et d'ame.
          Si vous depri,
Douce dame, qu'aiez de moy merci;                              505
Car vraiement, je morray d'amer ci,
Se de vo cuer, qui a le mien nerci,
          N'ay aligence.'

Et quant einsi li os dit ma grevance,
Un pou muer vi sa douce samblance,                             510
Ce me fu vis; dont je fui en doubtance
          D'estre escondis;
Mais ses regars m'asseüroit toudis,
Et sa douceur et son gracieus ris,

486. A lie--497. A requerir--511. AFM je fu

22

So weak, so beaten, so weary and full of anguish,
So troubled, so trembling, so shamefaced                    470
Was my heart, and with lovesickness
            So grievously infected
That no reason, direction, or wit remained in it;
Instead it was as if transformed and ravished,
When clearly, face to face, I could see                     475
            Her pure beauty.
Then was my heart stung
With an amorous sting, pricked with a joyful point,
And nourished with sweet nourishment
            By Sweet Thoughts,                               480
Who made my pains all stop
And made me hope for cure.
Thus often I had for love's sake
            Both joy and torture.
And so I remained in this way for a long time,              485
One hour happy and sorrowful the next,
So that I never dared to seek relief
            For what I suffered.
Nonetheless this great distress for love,
This burning desire, this cruel languor,                    490
In which I remained for many days,
            Her Fair Welcome,
The hope of ending my pain,
Her great beauty, her sweet, smiling grey eyes,
And the fact that in her there was no whit of pride,        495
            All these gave me
The strength to beg for mercy
Like a coward. Humbly I said to her, with
My color changed, and fearfully:
            'My lady dear,                                   500
Your beauty burns, inflames my heart,
So much that I love you above all else, without impure thoughts,
With my heart, my body, with true desire and soul.
            So I beg you,
Sweet lady, have mercy on me;                               505
For truly, I will die of loving thus,
If from your heart, which has afflicted mine,
            I have no relief.'

And when in this way I had dared tell her my grief,
I saw her sweet expression slightly change,                 510
So I thought; therefore I was in fear
            Of being shamed.
Yet all the time her look assured me,
And her sweetness and her gracious laugh

Si que par euls encor fui enhardis                                    515
          De dire: 'Helas!
Gentil dame, pour Dieu, n'ociez pas
Vostre loial ami, qui en vos las
Est si laciez qu'il en pert tout solas
          Et toute joie.'                                             520
Lors se treï vers moy la simple et coie,
Pour qui Amours me destreint et maistroie,
Et dist: 'Amis, certes, riens ne vorroie
          Faire a nelui,
Dont il eüst grevance ne anui;                                        525
Ne l'en ne doit faire chose a autrui
Qu'on ne vosist que l'en feïst a lui.
          Et, biaus amis,
Il n'est nuls biens qui ne soit remeris,
N'il n'est aussi maus qui ne soit punis.                             530
Si que, s'Amours vous a d'amer espris,
          Son guerredon
Vous en rendra en temps et en saison,
Se vous l'amez sans penser traïson.                                  [13r]
Et s'elle vous trouvoit autre que bon,                               535
          Ne doubtez mie
Qu'elle ne fust vo mortel anemie,
Ne que jamais garison ne aïe
Vous fust par li donnee, n'ottroïe
          De vos dolours.                                            540
Si que, biau sire, alez devers Amours,
Si li faites vos plains et vos clamours;
Car en li gist vos mors et vos secours,*
          Nom pas en moy.
Et pas ne sui cause de vostre anoy,                                  545
Ce m'est avis, si que souffrir m'en doy.
Plus ne vous say que dire, en bonne foy:
          Adieu vous di.'


Adont de moy la belle se parti
Qui de si grant doleur me reparti                                    550
Que par un po que mes cuers ne parti
          De son depart.
Mais la douceur de son plaisant regart
Par son dous art fist que j'en os regart;
Qu'au departir de moy, se Diex me gart,                              555
          Si doucement
Me regarda qu'il m'iert vis proprement
Que ses regars me disoit vraiement:
'Amis, je t'aim trés amoureusement.'
          Si que je fu                                               560


515. AFDKJ fu--543. FMC ou vos secours

24

So that by these I was emboldened enough                                515
        To cry 'Alas!
Gentle lady, for the sake of God, don't kill
Your faithful lover, who in your snares
Is caught so tight that he's lost all solace
        And all joy.'                                                     520
Then she drew toward me, that serene and quiet girl,
For whom Love tortured and abused me
And said: 'Friend, surely I would never
        Do to anyone
What might cause him grief or pain;                                      525
For one should not do to others
What he would not have done to him.
        And, sweet friend,
There is no good deed that is unrewarded,
Nor any evil one that is unpunished.                                     530
Thus, if Love has incited you to love,
        Her reward
She'll give you for it, in her time and season,
If you love her with no thoughts of trickery.
And if she finds you other than good,                                    535
        Don't doubt at all
That she'll become your mortal enemy,
And that no help or cure
Will be granted you by her, or given
        For your pains.                                                    540
Therefore, fair sir, present yourself to Love,
And to her rehearse your moans and cries,
For in her lie  your rescue and your death,
        But not in me;
I am not the cause of your discomfort                                    545
(Or so it seems to me) and should not suffer for it.
In good faith, I cannot tell you any more:
        I say goodbye.'

At this that beauty took her leave from me,
She who had portioned out such pain to me                                550
That my heart nearly broke
        With her departure.
But the sweetness of her pleasant look
With its sweet craftiness made me dare look at her;
So that as she left (may God protect me)
        So sweetly                                                          555
She did look my way that it truly seemed
That her expression actually said:
'Lover, I love you very much in Love's own way.'
        Therefore I was                                                    560

Tous confortez par la noble vertu
De ce regart qui puis m'a tant valu
Qu'il m'a toudis norri et soustenu
   En bon espoir.
Et s'il ne fust, certeinnement j'espoir    565
Que je fusse cheüs en desespoir,
Mais riens qui soit ne me feïst doloir
   Quant ses regars
Estoit seur moy en sousriant espars,
Si que, ma dame, einsi de toutes pars   570
Me confortoit et aidoit ses regars
   De ma dolour.

La demouray tous seuls en grant frëour,
Si qu'en pensant commensay son atour,
Sa grant douçour, sa colour, sa valour   575
   A remirer,
Son biau maintieng, son venir, son aler,
Son gentil corps, son gracieus parler,
Son noble port, son plaisant regarder,
   Et son viaire,     580
Qui tant estoit dous, humble, et debonnaire
Que de toute biauté fu l'exemplaire.
Et quant j'eus tout remiré son affaire,
   Certes, j'avoie
Moult grant deduit et moult parfaite joie,  585
Et pour trés boneüreus me tenoie,
Pour ce, sans plus, que loiaument l'amoie.
   Si que depuis
A li servir sui si tournez et duis,
Qu'en li servir s'est mis tous mes deduis,  590
N'autre labour ailleurs faire ne puis.
   Si la servi,
Amay, celay, doubtay, et oubeï
Moult longuement, que riens ne me meri.
Mais en la fin tant l'amay et chieri   595
   Qu'elle vit bien
Que je tendoie a s'onneur et son bien,
Et que mes cuers l'amoit sus toute rien;
Si que tant fis qu'elle me tint pour sien
   En tel maniere    600
Que de bon cuer riant, a lie chiere,
Me dist: 'Amis, vesci t'amie chiere
Qui plus ne vuet envers toy estre fiere,
   Qu'Amours le vuet,
Qui de bon cuer ad ce faire m'esmuet;   605
Et vraiement, estre autrement ne puet,

598. Other MSS seur

26

All comforted by the noble power
Of that look which since has proved so precious
That it has always nourished and sustained me
    In a good hope.
And had it not been so, I can only think        565
That I would have fallen into despair,
But nothing on earth could make me feel pain
    When her glance
In a smile had settled on me,
So that, my lady, in every way        570
Her look comforted me and aided me
    In my distress.

There in great turmoil I remained alone,
And thus began in my thoughts to marvel at
Her bearing, her great sweetness, her complexion,    575
    And her courage,
Her fair appearance, her arrival, her departure,
Her noble body, her gracious speech,
Her gentle carriage, her pleasant look
    And her image,        580
Which was so sweet, so serene, and debonaire
That she was the model for all beauty.
And when I had marvelled at all of her conduct,
    I had, to be sure,
Much great delight and much perfect joy,    585
And considered myself so very fortunate,
Because, to say it all, I loved her loyally.
    And so afterwards
I was so bent, so dedicated to serving her
That in this serving I found all my delight;    590
No other labor could I then perform.
    And so I served her,
Loved, protected, feared, obeyed her
For a very long time, and nothing was my reward.
At the last, however, I loved and cherished her so much
    That she saw well
That I intended only honor for her and her good,
And also that my heart did love her above all else;
And so I did so much that she took me for her own
    In such a way        600
That with a good and happy heart, a pleasant face,
She told me: 'Lover, you see here your own dear love
Who no longer wishes to act haughtily toward you,
    Since Love desires it,
Who with good heart has moved me to this;    605
And truly, it cannot be otherwise,

Car moult grant chose a en faire l'estuet;*
     Pour ce m'amour
Avec mon cuer vous doin, sans nul retour;
Si vous depri que vous gardez m'onnour,          610
Car je vous aim dessus tous et honnour.'
     Et quant je vi
Que ma dame m'appelloit son amy
Si doucement, et que le dous ottri
M'avoit donné de s'amour, sans nul si,       [13v]  615
     Se je fui liez,
Douce dame, ne vous en mervilliez;
Car j'estoie devant desconsilliez,
Povres, perdus, despris, et essiliez,
     Sans nul ressort,                 620
Quant je failloie a son trés dous confort.
Mais recouvrez, ressuscitez de mort,
Riche au dessus, pleins de grant reconfort,
     Et sans anoy
Fui, quant me dist: 'Amis, a ti m'ottroy     625
De trés bon cuer.' Et ce trés dous ottroy
Cent mille fois me fist plus grant qu'un roy;
     Si que la joie
Ne porroit nuls raconter que j'avoie.
Car tant fui liez que je ne l'en pooie      630
Remercier ne parler ne savoie.
     Mais en la fin,
Com fins loiaus amoureus, de cuer fin,
Espris d'amer, sans penser mal engin,
Moult humblement li dis, le chief enclin,    635
     Et sans effroy:
'Dame que j'aim plus qu'autre, ne que moy,
En qui sens, temps, cuer, vie, amour employ,
Tant com je puis, nom pas tant com je doy,
     Vous remercy               640
Dou noble don de vo douce merci,
Car tant m'avez puisamment enrichi,
Tant resjoï, si gari, tant meri,
     Que vraiement,
Se quanqu'il a dessous le firmament      645
Et quanqu'il fu et sera, quittement
Me fust donnez pour faire mon talent,
     Je ne l'amasse
Tant de cent pars, que je fais vostre grace.
Si pri a Dieu que jamais ne mefface     650
Chose envers vous qui nostre amour efface,
     Et que vo vueil
Puisse acomplir, einsi com je le vueil

For I must undertake a great and serious thing;
        Since my love
I present you with my heart, never to be retrieved;
And so I beg you to guard my honor well,        610
For I love you more than honor and all else.'
        And when I saw
That my lady named me her lover
So sweetly, and had the sweet present of her love
Bestowed on me, without a 'but,'        615
        If I was happy then,
Sweet lady, don't wonder at it;
For until that moment I had been discouraged,
Deprived, lost, exiled, and despoiled,
        Beyond relief,        620
When I had lacked her very sweet comfort,
But now I was recovered, brought back
From death, rich beyond belief, filled with great comfort,
        And without grief
Was I, when she told me: 'Lover, I grant myself to you  625
With a very good heart.' And this very sweet boon
Made me a hundred thousand times grander than a king;
        So that the joy
I had no one could describe.
For I was so happy that I could not        630
Utter my thanks for it or speak or think.
        But in the end,
Like a lover loyal and courtly, with a noble heart,
Inflamed with loving, without a devious thought,
Very humbly, with lowered head, I told her,        635
        Without difficulty:
'Lady, whom I love above all others, indeed myself,
In whom I have placed all my reason, heart, time, life, and love,
As far as I have power to, but not as much as I ought,
        I thank you        640
For the noble gift of your sweet mercy,
Since you have most greatly enriched me,
So elated, so cured, so rewarded me,
        That truly,
If everything that exists beneath the sky        645
Or all that was or will be
Was given me entirely to do my will,
        I would not value it
A hundredth part as much as I prize your grace.
And so I pray God that I may never wrong you        650
In anything that might destroy our love,
        And also that your will
I might fulfill, just as I hope I can

Faire--humblement, sans hautesse, n'orgueil--
Car, se je puis, assez mieus que ne sueil,                    655
      Vous serviray
Trés loiaument de cuer, et ameray,
Et vostre honneur en tous cas garderay,
N'en dit, n'en fait, n'en penser ne feray
      Chose envers vous,                                660
N'envers autrui dont vous aiez courrous;
Einsois serez ma dame et mes cuers dous,
Mes dieus terriens, aourez dessus tous;
      Et sans doubtance,
Se je fais riens contre vostre plaisence,                      665
Ne dont vos cuers ait courrous ne grevance,
Sachiez de voir que c'iert par negligence.'
      Ma dame, einsi
La merciay com vous avez oÿ,
Dou noble don de sa douce merci.                               670
Et elle aussi me jura et plevi
      Moult durement
Qu'a tous jours mais m'ameroit loiaument,
Sans moy guerpir et sans departement.
Eins regnay en joie longuement,                                675
      Que je n'avoie
Nulle chose qui fust contraire a joie,
Mais envoisiez et reveleus estoie,
Jolis et gais, trop plus que ne soloie;
      Et c'estoit drois                                 680
Qu'a mon pooir fusse gens et adrois,
Car par cuidier estoie en tous endrois
Li mieus amez des amans et li rois.
      Mais quant Fortune,
La desloial, qui n'est pas a tous une,                         685
M'ot si haut mis, com mauvaise et enfrune,
Moy ne mes biens ne prisa une prune;
      Einsi fist la moe,
Moy renoia et me tourna la joe;
Quant elle m'ot assis dessus sa roe,                           690
Puis la tourna, si cheï en la boe.
      Mais ce fist elle,
La traïtre, toudis preste et isnelle
De ceaus traïr qu'elle met dessous s'ele
Pour ce que Dieus et Nature la bele,           *[14r]*   695
      Quant il formerent
Celle que j'aim, si fort se deliterent
En la trés grant biauté qu'il li donnerent
Que loyauté a mettre y oublierent.
      Et bien y pert!                                   700


675. A resnay--693. F traite

Humbly, not haughtily, not proudly--
For, if I'm able, much better than has been my custom    655
        I'll serve you
Quite loyally with my heart, and love you,
And in all things I'll keep well your honor;
Not in word, or deed, or in thought
        Against you                                      660
Or against anyone will I do anything to make you angry.
Instead you'll be my lady and my sweetheart,
My god on earth, adored above all others;
        And without a doubt,
If I do anything against your pleasure,                 665
Something which would give your heart anger or grief,
Know truly that this would be through negligence alone.'
        My lady, in this way
I thanked her, as you have heard,
For the noble gift of her sweet mercy.                  670
And she also pledged to me and swore
        Very adamantly
That she would always love me loyally,
Without forsaking or deserting me.
And so a long time I held sway in joy,                  675
        So that I had
Nothing that was contrary to joy;
Instead I was pleased and full of celebration,
Jolly and gay, much more so than I'd ever been.
        And it was right                                680
That to my best ability I was kind and thoughtful,
Since, it seemed, I was in every place
The best loved of lovers and the king.
        But when Fortune,
The disloyal one, who is never the same to all,         685
Had lifted me up so high, like one both evil and miserly,
She began to value me and mine not worth a plum.
        Instead she mocked me,
Denied me, turned her face away;
After she had seated me upon her wheel,                 690
She turned it, and then I tumbled into the mud.
        But she did this,
That traitress, quick and ready at all times
To betray those whom she puts beneath her wing,
Because God and beautiful Nature,                       695
        When they shaped
The one I love, so greatly delighted
In the incredible beauty that they gave her
That they forgot to put faithfulness in her.
        And what a loss!                                700

31

Que je say bien et voy tout en apert
Que ma dame, qui tant a corps apert,
Que mes cuers crient, aime, obeïst, et sert,
   A fait amy
Nouvelement, sans cause, autre que mi.      705
Si que, dame, se je pleure et gemy
Parfondement et di souvent: 'Aimy!'
   N'est pas merveille,
Quant sa fine biauté qui n'a pareille
Et sa colour vive, fresche, et vermeille,      710
Et son trés dous regart qui me traveille,
   M'ont eslongié,
Et qu'elle m'a dou tout donne congié
Et de tous biens privé et estrangié.
Helas!   Comment aroie je cuer lié?      715
   Et a grant tort
M'a retollu ma joie et mon confort,
Et si m'a mis en si grant desconfort
Que je say bien que j'en aray la mort;
   Ne riens deffendre      720
Ne m'en porroit, nès i. seul confort rendre.
Mais ce qui fait mon cuer partir et fendre,
C'est ce que je ne me say a qui prendre
   De mon anui,
Car il m'est vis, se par Fortune sui      725
Jus dou degré ou jadis montez fui,
Par li en qui je ne me fi, n'apui,
   A dire voir,
Que nul mal gré ne li en doy savoir,
Car elle fist dou faire son devoir;      730
N'elle ne doit autre mestier avoir
   Fors de traïr
Ceaus qu'elle voit monter et enrichir, *
Et de faire le bas en haut venir;
N'elle ne puet personne tant chierir      735
   Que seurté
Li face avoir de sa bonneürté,
Soit de joie, soit de maleürté,
Que sus ou jus ne l'ait moult tost hurté.
   C'est sa nature:      740
Si bien ne sont fors que droite aventure;
Ce n'est qu'uns vens, une fausse estature;
Une joie est qui po vaut et po dure;
   C'est fols s'i fie!
Chascun deçoit et nelui ne deffie.      745
Et se je di que la mort qui m'aigrie
Puis demander a ma dame jolie,

715. CDKJP aroie le--733. CDKJP fait monter

For I know well and have clearly seen
That my lady, who has such a lovely appearance,
Whom my heart fears, loves, obeys, and serves,
        Has taken a lover
Recently, without reason, someone other than me.      705
And so, lady, if I moan and cry
Very bitterly and often say 'Oh no!'
        It is no wonder,
Since her pure beauty which has no equal,
Her vibrant complexion, fresh, and rosy,      710
And that sweet look which tortures me still,
        Have deserted me,
And she's said her last goodbye,
And deprived and estranged me from every good.
Alas! How could I have a happy heart?      715
        And very wrongfully
She's taken back my joy and comfort,
And so has put me in such great distress
That I know well I'll have my death in it.
        Nor can anything      720
Save me from this, or render me a single comfort.
But what rends and cuts my heart in two
Is that I do not know whom to blame
        For my grief,
Since it seems that if by Fortune I      725
Was removed from the stairs I once had climbed,
Through Fortune in whom I place no trust, do not depend on,
        Then to tell the truth
I ought to feel no bitterness toward Fortune for this,
Since in her deed she simply did her duty,      730
And she ought to have no other task
        But to betray
Those she sees mount up, succeed,
And to raise up those of low estate;
Nor can Fortune love a person so dearly      735
        That she'd issue
Any guarantee for him to keep his luck,
Whether it's for joy or pain,
Namely that she wouldn't suddenly hurl him up or down.
        Such is her nature:      740
And so goods are nothing but lucky happenstance,
And this is only a breeze, a deceptive shape.
Joy is that which hardly lasts and is of little worth.
        He's a fool who trusts to it!
It deceives and defies everyone.      745
And if I say that this death which sickens me
I can blame on my pretty lady,

```
                Par quel raison
Le feray je, ne par quel occoison?
Elle s'est mise en la subjection                              750
D'Amours, a qui elle a fait de li don
                Entierement,
Et vuet qu'elle ait trés souvereinnement,
Com ses souvreins, seur li commandement
Si qu'el ne puet contrester nullement                        755
                A son plaisir;
Eins li couvient en tous cas oubeïr.
Dont, se ma dame a plaisence et desir
De moy laissier pour un autre enchierir,
                Ce fait Amour,                               760
Nom pas ma dame, en qui tout a valour;
Car elle fait son devoir et s'onnour
D'obeïr a son souverein signour.
                Si qu'il m'est vis,
Quant par Amour d'amer estoie espris,                        765
Qu'en ce faisant Amours a plus mespris
Par devers moy que ma dame de pris,
                C'est a entendre,
S'Amours pooit par devers moy mesprendre.
Mais nullement je ne puis ce comprendre,                     770
Car longuement, com douce mere et tendre
                M'a repeü
De ses dous biens au mieus qu'elle a peü,
Ne je n'ay pas encor aperceü,
Pour nul meschief que j'aie receü,                           775
                Que tout adès                         [14v]
Elle ne m'ait com amie esté près
Et qu'el ne m'ait servi de tous mes mès,
De plours devant et de souspirs après.
                C'est ma viande;                            780
Mon appetit plus ne vuet ne demande,
Ne, par m'ame, riens n'est a quoy je tende
Fors seulement a ce que mes cuers fende.
                Einsi Amour
Croist en mon cuer au fuer de ma dolour,                     785
Ne ne s'en part, ne de nuit, ne de jour,
Eins me compaingne en mon dolereus plour
                Par sa bonté;
Si que je di que c'est grant amisté
Qui m'a esté mere en prosperité,                             790
Et encor est en mon adversité.
                Si ne me puis
Pleindre de li, se trop mauvais  ne suis,
Car sans partir de moy toudis la truis,
```

                    By what reasoning
Would I do this, and for what cause?
She was made subject to the rule                              750
Of Love, to whom she gave herself
                    Completely,
And wished that Love would rule her
Just as her sovereign, wished to be under her command,
So that she could not at all resist                           755
                    What was Love's pleasure:
Instead she always found it necessary to obey.
Thus, if it was my lady's pleasure or desire
To desert me in order to love another man,
                    Love did this,                            760
Not my lady, in whom all things are worthy;
For she did her duty and what was honor:
To obey her sovereign lord.
                    And so it seems to me,
When I was inflamed by Love to love,                          765
That Love, so doing, did more wrong
To me than my worthy lady did,
                    And that means
That Love indeed could do me wrong.
But this I cannot comprehend at all,                          770
Since, for a long time, like a sweet and tender mother,
                    She nourished me
With her sweet goods as best she could,
Nor did I then yet perceive,
For any hurt I got,                                           775
                    That always
She had not been like a friend at my side,
And that she had not served me with all her courses,
With tears as appetizers, sighing as dessert.
                    This is my meat;                          780
My appetite does not wish or ask for more,
Yet, by my soul, now I'm drawn toward nothing,
Save that which breaks my heart.
                    And therefore Love
Grows in my heart in proportion to my pain,                  785
Nor does she leave, not by night, not by day,
But is my companion in my painful weeping
                    Because of her goodness.
And so I maintain that she's a great friend
Who in prosperity was my mother                              790
And still in adversity remains the same.
                    So I cannot
Complain of her, unless I want to be very wicked,
For I have always found her at my side,

Ne je ne suis mie par li destruis,                        795
        Qu'elle ne puet
Muer les cuers, puis que Dieus ne le vuet.
Car quant Dieus fist ma dame qui me suet
Clamer amy, dont li cuers trop me duet,
        S'il et Nature,                                   800
Quant il firent sa biauté fine et pure,
Plaisant a tous seur toute creature,
Eüssent lors en sa douce figure
        Loyauté mis,
Je fusse encor appellez ses amis,                         805
Et ses cuers qui tant bien m'avoit promis
N'eüst jamais esté mes anemis.
        Pour ce di qu'en ce
Nature et Dieus feïrent ignorance,
Sauve l'onneur d'eaus et leur reverence,                  810
Quant il firent si trés belle samblance
        Sans loiauté.
Car s'elle eüst cent fois meins de biauté,
Et elle fust loial, la grant bonté
De loiauté l'eüst plus honnouré                           815
        Que s'elle fust
Cent mille fois plus bele, et mieus pleüst,
Et en tous cas trop mieus plaire deüst,
Pour ce qu'en li riens a dire n'eüst.
        Si que je croy                                    820
Qu'a Bonne Amour, a Fortune, n'a soy
Riens demander de mes dolours ne doy.
Et en puis je riens demander a moy?
        Certes oïl!
Car je me mis de richesse en essil,                       825
De seürté en un mortel peril,
De joie en dueil, par son regart soutil,
        Et de franchise
En servitute ou on n'aimme, ne prise
Moy, ne mes biens, m'amour, ne mon servise,*             830
Ne ma vie vaillant une cerise.
        Et nompourquant,
Il m'est avis que pas ne mespris, quant
Je l'enamay, qu'en ce monde vivant
N'avoit dame qui fust si excellent,                       835
        Ce disoit on.
Si devins siens en bonne entention,
Ne jamais n'i cuidasse, se bien non,
Pour la grandeur de son trés bon renon,
        Qui m'a destruit.                                 840
Mais ce n'est pas tout d'or quanque reluit*

830. F ne monnour--841. AFMC quanqui

Nor am I destroyed in any way by her,                              795
        For she cannot
Alter hearts, since God does not wish this.
But when God made the lady who was accustomed
To call me lover, for whom my heart pains me too much,
        If He and Nature,                                         800
When they created her noble and pure beauty,
Pleasing to all men beyond all other creatures,
Had they then in that sweet form
        Put loyalty,
I would yet be called her lover,                                  805
And her heart which promised me so very much
Would never have become my foe.
        So I say in this
That God and Nature acted ignorantly
(Saving their honor and the respect due to them)                 810
When they fashioned such a pretty form
        Without loyalty.
For if she'd had a hundred times less beauty,
And she had been loyal, the great virtue
Of loyalty would have honored her much more                      815
        Than if she'd been
A hundred thousand times more beautiful, and she'd have pleased
More, and it's a fact she would have pleased more
Because there would have been nothing in her to fault.
        And so I believe                                         820
That not to Good Love, not to Fortune, not to my lady
Should I assign the blame for my sorrows.
And then can I blame myself in any way for them?
        Surely yes!
For I exiled myself from riches,                                 825
Went from safety into mortal peril,
From joy to pain, through her subtle look,
        And from freedom
Into a slavery where no one loves or treasures
Me, or my honor, love, or service,                               830
Or even my precious life, as much as a cherry.
        And nonetheless
It seems that I did no wrong
When I fell in love, since in this living world
There was no lady who was so excellent,                          835
        So it was said.
So I became hers with good intention,
And never hoped for anything from it, except good,
Because of the grandeur of her most impressive fame,
        Which has destroyed me.                                  840
No, all that glitters is not gold,

37

N'on ne doit pas tant amer son deduit
Qu'on ne s'en puist retraire, quant il cuit.
      Et se je fusse
Tous li mieudres dou mont, je n'esleüsse 845
Autre que li, ne mieus je ne peüsse,
Se loyauté en li trouve eüsse.
      Si ne m'en say
Que demander et a qui m'en penray
Des griés doleurs et des meschiés que j'ay. 850
S'on m'en demande, a tous responderay
      Que ç'a fait Dieus
Et Nature; dont c'est meschiés et dieus,
Quant il firent son corps en trestous lieus
Si bel, si gent, si dous, qu'on ne puet mieus, 855
      S'il fust loiaus. *[15r]*
Si me penray a eaus deus de mes maus?
Je non feray, car il me sont trop haus;
Eins soufferray, c'est mes milleurs consaus
      D'ore en avant. 860


Or vous ay dit la maniere comment
Amours me fist estre loial amant,
L'estat, la guise, et tout le couvenant,
      Ce qui m'avint,
Comment pris fui, comment on me retint, 865
Comment de moy ma dame ne souvint,
Les biens, les maus qu'endurer me couvint
      Jusqu'au jour d'hui,
Comment je n'ay aïe de nelui,
Comment vengier ne puis mon grief anui, 870
Dont a par mi me mourdri et destrui
      Si que je di,
Se bien m'avez entendu et oÿ,
Que la doleur dont en morant langui,
Qui mon viaire a desteint et pali 875
      Par sa rigour,
Est de vos maus cent mille fois gringnour;
Car fine joie et parfaite douçour
Sont vostre mal encontre la dolour
      Qui me martire." 880
"Certes, sire, pas ne vous vueil desdire
Que vous n'aiez moult de dolour et d'ire,
S'einsi perdez ce que vos cuers desire.
      Mais toute voie,
Il m'est avis, et dire l'oseroie, 885
Consideré vo dolour et la moie,
Qu'il a en vous meins dolour et plus joie

849. KJ ne a qui men plaindray--871. A mourdris--877. A
grignour

38

And one should not love his joy so much
That he cannot abandon it, when he thinks to.
       And if I had been
The greatest man in the world, I would not have picked  845
Anyone but her, nor could I have done better,
If I had found loyalty in her.
       So I do not know
What to ask for or from whom
About the grievous pain and misfortune I bear.  850
If I were asked, to all I'd answer
       That God and Nature
Did it; for it was misadventure and sorrow
When they made her body in every way
So beautiful, so noble, so soft, that no one could do better,
       If it had been loyal.
Should I call these two to account for my woes?
I won't do it, for they are too high for me;
Instead I'll endure; that's my best course
       From now on.  860

Now I have told you the way in which
Love made a true lover of me,
The circumstance, the means, and all that was agreed,
       That which happened to me,
How I was taken, how I was held,  865
How my lady does not remember me,
The joys, the sorrows I must endure
       Until this very day,
How I have had the help of no one,
How I could not avenge my grievous hurt,  870
Which greatly harms, destroys me.
       And so I say,
If you have listened closely and heard me well,
That the pain in which I languish, dying,
Which has disfigured me and made me pale  875
       By its harshness,
Is greater by a hundred thousand times than your pain;
For tender joy and perfect sweetness
Are your ills measured against the pain
       That martyrs me."  880
"Certainly, sir, I wish not to deny
That you have a great deal of pain and anger,
Thus to have lost her whom your heart desires.
       But nonetheless,
It seems to me, and I dare say it,  885
Considering your pain and mine,
That there's less hurt in you and more joy

```
              Qu'il n'ait en moy.
Si vous en vueil dire raison pourquoy;
Vous m'avez dit que vous amez en foy                    890
Ceste dame qui tant vous fait d'anoy
              Et amerez
De loial cuer, tant comme vis serez.
Et puisqu'il est einsi que vous l'amez,
Certes, je croy que s'amour desirez,                    895
              Car avenir
Voy po souvent qu'amours soit sans desir,
Ne que desirs d'amours se puist souffrir
D'esperence; et s'avez souvenir
              Aucune fois                                900
Dont, quant vos cuers est par desir destrois,
Il vous souvient de la bele aus crins blois,
Dont vous avez des pensers plus de trois.
              Si ne puet estre
Que vous n'aiez aucun penser qui nestre                 905
Aucune joie face en vous, qui remestre
Fait la dolour qui si vous tient a mestre,
              Si qu'a la fie
Par souvenir avez pensée lie
Qui vo dolour espart et entroublie;                     910
Mais la mienne jour et nuit monteplie
              Sans nul sejour,
Et toudis croist li ruissaus de mon plour,
N'avoir ne puis pensée par nul tour,
N'esperence de recouvrer m'amour.                       915
              Mais par servir,
Par honnourer, par celer, par cremir,
Par endurer liement et souffrir,
Par bien amer de cuer et oubeïr
              Trés humblement                            920
Povez encore avoir aligement,
Joie et l'amour de celle ou vos cuers tent.
Si que je di que j'ay plus de tourment,
              Et moult visible
Est la raison, ce m'est vis, et sensible:               925
Car de ravoir vo dame, c'est possible;
Mais mon ami ravoir, c'est impossible
              Selonc nature."
"Dame, d'onneur, de sens, et de mesure
A plus en vous qu'en autre creature;                    930
Car par vo sens mis a desconfiture
              Moult tost seroie,
S'a vos raisons respondre ne pooie.
Car vraiement, faire ne le saroie
```

933. MCBDKJ ne sauoie

                Than there is in me.
So I wish to give you my reason why;
You've told me that you have faithfully loved          890
That lady who has given you so much distress,
                And that you'll love her
With a loyal heart, as long as you're alive.
And since you love her in this way,
Surely I believe that you desire her love,             895
                For very seldom
I have seen it happen for love to exist without desire,
Nor that desire for love could endure
Without hope; and if you have memory
                At any time,                            900
Then, when your heart is devastated by desire,
It recalls to you the beauty with blonde hair,
And from this you have more thoughts than three.
                Then it cannot be
That you never have a single thought which makes       905
Joy grow in you, which makes subside
The pain that so tightly binds you,
                So that in the end
Through memory you ·have happy thoughts
Which shove the sorrow out and make you forget it.     910
But mine breeds by day and night
                Without a rest,
And every day the streams of my tears increase,
And I can't have a thought in any way,
Nor a hope of recovering my love.                      915
                But by serving,
By honoring, by keeping secret, by fearing,
By happily enduring and suffering,
By loving well from the heart and obeying
                Very humbly                             920
You still can have relief,
Joy, and the love of her toward whom your heart inclines.
And so I say that I have more torment,
                And quite evident
Is the reason, it seems to me, and sound:              925
For to have your lady back is possible;
But to have my lover back is impossible
                According to Nature."
"Lady, there's more honor, wisdom,
And moderation in you than in any other creature;      930
But by your reasoning I would be dismayed
                Very quickly,
If I could not respond to your arguments.
But truly I cannot accomplish this

Si sagement, com mestier en aroie.                          935
       Mais repeter
Vueil vos raisons, se j'y puis assener.
Vous arguëz que j'aimme sans fausser                        [15v]
Et ameray, tant com porray durer,
       Sans repentir;                          940
Et puis que j'aim, il faut qu'aie desir
Qui ne se puet deporter ne souffrir
D'esperence; et si ay souvenir,
       Qui esmouvoir
Me fait souvent a maint penser avoir.                       945
Certes, dame, ce vous ottroi pour voir,
Fors seulement que je n'ay point d'espoir.
       Mais sachiez bien,
Dame, comment qu'il n'ait partout que bien,
Qu'en ce vostre entendement et le mien                      950
Ne se joingnent, ne acordent en rien;
       Eins sont contraire;
Einsi com je le vous pense a retraire,
Quant poins sera.  Mais ce ne vueil pas taire
Que vous dites qu'encor puis je tant faire                  955
       Par honnourer,
Par bien servir, par souffrir, par doubter,
Par oubeïr, par loiaument amer,
Qu'en joie puis ma dame recouvrer;
       Mais ce seroit                          960
Moult grant maistrie au garder qui l'aroit.
Car en un lieu son cuer n'arresteroit
Nès que feroit un estuef seur un toit.
       Et vostre amour,
Qui tant avoit de pris et de valour,                        965
Ne povez mais recouvrer par nul tour,
Dont vous avez veinne et pale coulour.
       Si qu'einsis dites
Que mes dolours sont assez plus petites
Que les vostres, dont je ne sui pas quites,                 970
Ne que pas n'ay acquis par mes merites.
       Si respondray
A ces raisons au mieus que je porray,
Et sus chascune un po m'arresteray;
Si en diray ce que j'en sens et say                         975
       De sentement.

Dame, il est voirs que j'aim trés loiaument
Ce qui me het, c'est ma dame au corps gent,
Qui est ma mort et mon destruisement
       Quant je li voy*                         980

980-3. These verses are found only in CEKJPR.

42

As wisely as I might have need.                                    935
            But I wish
To repeat your reasons, if I can bring it off.
You argue that I love without deceit
And will love, as long as I may last,
            Without repenting;                                      940
And since I love, I must have desire,
Which cannot do without nor bypass
Hope; and so I have memories,
            Which often
Move me to having many thoughts.                                   945
Certainly, lady, I grant you this is true,
Except only that I have no hope at all.
            But mark well,
Lady, despite our good intentions in this matter,
That your understanding and mine of it                             950
Do not meet, do not agree in anything;
            Instead they contradict,
And so I think to make you withdraw yours,
When the time is right. But I will not pass by
In silence your statement that I still can do much                 955
            By honoring,
By serving well, by suffering, by fearing,
By obeying, by loving loyally,
So that in joy I can get my lady back.
            But this would be                                       960
A very great feat for the man who had to undertake it.
For in one place his heart would not remain,
No more than a ball does on a roof.
            And your love,
Who was so strong and worthy,                                      965
You cannot recover in any way,
And thus your complexion's weak and pale.
            And so you say therefore
That my pains are much less
Than yours; and so I am not paid,                                  970
Nor have I earned anything by my merits.
            So I will answer
Your points as best I can,
And I'll stop a little over each one;
Also I'll tell what I feel and know about them                     975
            According to my sentiments.

Lady, it is true that I love very loyally
The woman who hates me, that is, my lady of the noble form,
Who is my death and my destruction
            When I see her                                          980

Autrui amer, et n'a cure de moy,
Qu'elle deüst amer en bonne foy;
Si qu'a peinne que tout ne me marvoy
    De ceste amour.
Car, s'elle amast ma vie, ne m'onnour,           985
En la doleur ou je vif et demour
Ne me laissast languir l'eure d'un jour
    Pour tout le monde;
Mais en vertu font monteplier l'onde
De la doleur qui en mon cuer habonde:            990
Amours premiers et ma dame seconde.
    Pour ç'ay desir.
Mais quels est il?   Il est de tost morir,
Car il n'est riens qui me peüst venir
Dont je peüsse esperer le garir.                 995
    Et se j'avoie
L'amour de li miex que je ne soloie,
Ne say je pas se je m'i fieroie.
Certes, nennil!  Pourquoy?   Je n'oseroie.
    Car nourreture,                              1000
Si com on dit, veint et passe nature,
Et toudis va, s'il ne se desnature,
Li leus au bois; c'est la verité pure.
    Et par ce point
En mon desir d'esperance n'a point,              1005
Mais en li gist desespoir si apoint
Que je seray matez en l'angle point
    Dou souvenir,
Que vous dites, qui fait en moy venir
La pensée qui me fait resjoïr.                   1010
Certes, de lui ne puis jamais joïr,
    Ne n'en joï,
Ne ne le vi, ne senti, ne oï,
Puis que ma dame ot fait nouvel ami,
Car adonques se parti il de mi.                  1015
    Si vueil prouver
Que c'est la riens qui plus me puet grever
Et qui plus fait mon cuer desesperer
Que souvenir. Vous savez (et est cler;
    Chascuns le voit),                           1020
Que, se jamais il ne me souvenoit
De ma dame qui me tient si destroit,
Que ma doleur oubliée seroit.
    Et s'elle estoit
Oubliée, l'oubliance feroit                      1025
Qu'elle dou tout morroit ou cesseroit;
Et ce garir de tous maus me porroit.


1000-47. These verses are found only in CEKJPR.

Love another, and have no thought of me,
Whom she ought to love in good faith;
And so I am almost totally bewildered
          About this love.
For, if she loved my life or honor,                           985
In this pain where I live and dwell
She would not let me languish an hour of a day
          For all the world.
But with great force they increase the wave
Of suffering that overflows my heart:                         990
Love first, and my lady second.
          For this reason I have desire.
But what is it for? It is to die swiftly.
Since nothing can happen to me
From which I can hope for cure.                                995
          And if I had
Her love more than is now my lot,
I do not know if I would trust in it.
Surely not! Why? I wouldn't dare.
          For nurture,                                         1000
As one says, conquers and surpasses nature
And always, if he does not go against his kind,
The wolf will go to the woods; that's the pure truth.
          And for this reason
There is no hope at all in my desire,                         1005
But instead a despair so fierce lies in it
That I will be destroyed in the sharp corner
          Of memory,
Which, you said, makes come to me
The thought that makes me rejoice.                            1010
Surely, I can never take joy in it,
          Nor have I yet,
Nor have I seen it, not felt, not heard it,
Since my lady has taken a new lover,
For at that moment the thought parted from me.                1015
          So I wish to prove
That this is the thing that grieves me more
And which makes my heart despair more
Than memory. You know (and it's clear;
          Everyone sees it),                                   1020
That, if I never remembered
My lady who binds me so tightly to her,
My grief would be forgotten.
          And if she were
Forgotten, the forgetting would cause                         1025
It to die out completely or cease;
And this would cure me of all my sickness.

            Mais qu'avient il?
Cils souvenirs, par son engin soubtil,
Me ramentoit le viaire gentil                          1030
Et le gent corps pour qui mon cuer essil;
            Mès engendrez,
Nez et fenis est, et continuez
Tous en doleur. Pour quoy?   Pour ce qu'amez
Cuiday estre, quant amis fui clamez                     1035
            Trés doucement.
Helas! Dolens!  Or est bien autrement,
Quant ma dame aimme autre nouvellement.
Et puet on pis, dame, s'on ne se pent?
            Certes, nennil!                             1040
Car c'est pour mettre un amant a essil;
N'eschaper hors de si mortel peril
N'en devroit pas un d'entre cinq cent mil.
            Dont il avient
Par maintes fois, quant de ce me souvient,             1045
Que mes las cuers dedens mon corps devient
Si dolereus que pasmer me couvient.
            Et se pensée
Par souvenir est en moy engendrée,
Quelle est elle ? Elle est desconfortée,               1050
Triste, mourne, lasse, et desesperée.
            Et, par may foy,
Je n'ay penser qui ne soit contre moy;
Et si le pren au pis. Savez pour quoy?
Pour ce qu'aler ma dame en change voy.                 1055
            Et se la joie
Que j'avoie, quant en sa grace estoie,
Ne fust plus grant que dire ne saroie,
N'ymaginer ne penser ne porroie,
            La grief dolour                             1060
Qui me destreint en fust assez menour.
Mais de tant plus que j'eus joie grignour,
De tant est plus crueuse ma langour.
            Et que ravoir
Puisse ma dame, ou je n'ay nul espoir,                 1065
Ymaginer ne le puis, ne veöir.
Se vous diray ce qui m'i fait doloir:
            Dame, il me samble
Qu'une chose qui se part et assamble
En pluseurs lieus, et avec c'elle tramble*             1070
Et n'arreste ne que fueille de tramble,
            Et n'est estable,                           [16r]
Eins est toudis changant et variable,
Puis ci,  puis la, or au feu, a la table,

1055. FMCJ au change--1066. BDEK la--1070. A avec ce elle

46

                But would it happen?
This memory, by its subtle trickery,
Recalls to me the gentle form
And the noble body for whom my heart is splitting;                    1030
            Yet this memory is engendered,
Born and ended, and continued
All in suffering.  Why?    Because I think about
Being loved, since lover I was called                                 1035
            Very sweetly.
Alas!    Sorrowful!    Now it is quite otherwise,
When my lady newly loves another.
And could one do worse, lady, unless he hanged himself?
            Surely not!                                               1040
For this results in exile for a lover;
And not one man in five hundred thousand
Could escape from such a deadly danger.
            Thus it happens
Many times, when I remember this,                                     1045
That the sorrowing heart within my body becomes
So painful that I must faint.
            And if thought
Through memory is engendered in me,
What is it?   It is devoid of comfort,                                1050
Sad, mournful, sorrowful, and despairing.
            And by my faith,
I have no thought at all that's not against me;
And so I take all this for the worst.  Do you know why?
Because I see my lady alter.                                          1055
            And if the joy
That I had, when I was in her grace,
Was not much greater than I know how to describe,
Or could imagine or even think,
            Then the grievous pain                                    1060
Which grips me would be much less.
Since as much as I once had great joy,
In the same measure is my suffering intense.
            And that I could
Have my lady back, for which I have no hope,                          1065
I cannot imagine or conceive.
And I'll tell you what makes me hurt in this regard:
            Lady, it seems
That something which separates and comes together
In several places, and likewise shakes                               1070
And does not keep more still than an aspen leaf,
            And which is unstable,
Instead is always changing and variable,
Now here, now there, at the hearth, at the table,

Et puis ailleurs, c'est chose moult doubtable;    1075
          Car nullement
On ne la puet avoir seürement.
C'est droitement li gieus d'enchantement*
Que ce qu'on cuide avoir certeinnement,
          On ne l'a mie.                           1080
Einsi est il, dame, quoy que nuls die,
De ma dame, qui se change et varie,
Donne et retolt, or het, or est amie,
          N'en une part
N'est tous ses cuers, et s'aucuns y repart,        1085
Certes, je croy qu'il en a povre part,
Et que de li celle part tost se part.
          N'a droit jugier,
Amans ne puet avoir homme si chier
Qu'il le vosist avoir a parsonnier                 1090
En ses amours, sans plus, nès par cuidier.
          Et pour ç'a plein
Ne puis avoir son cuer, dont je me plain;
Car cuers qui va einsi de main en main,
S'on l'a ennuit, on ne l'a pas demain;             1095
          Et toute voie
Est vrais amans li drois oisiaus de proie,
Car il ne vuet avoir pour toute joie
Fors tout le cuer de celle ou il s'otroie.
          Si que je di                             1100
Que vous rariez aussi tost vostre ami,
Comme on avroit mué le cuer de li
Ad ce qu'il fust entierement en mi
          Mis sans retraire;
Car on ne puet le leu de sa piau traire            1105
Sans l'escorchier, n'on ne puet d'un buef faire
Un esprivier, ne aussi le contraire.
          Et, douce dame,
La coustume est partout d'omme et de fame
Que, quant dou corps s'est departie l'ame          1110
Et li corps est en terre sous la lame,
          Qu'en petit d'eure
Est oubliez, ja soit ce qu'on en pleure.
Car nuls n'en voy ne nulle qui demeure*
Tant en son pleur qu'a joie ne requeure,           1115
          Eins que li ans
Soit acomplis, tant soit loiaus amans,
Ne excepter n'en vueil petis ne grans.
Et vraiement, je croy que ce soit sens.
          Si en ferez                              1120
La coustume; pas ne la briserez

1078. ADEKJP le gieu--1102. F aroit--1114. AFMBKJ nuls

48

And then elsewhere, that's a very uncertain thing;          1075
          For in no way
Can any man possess it securely.
It must truly be the play of a spell
That the thing one believes to have for certain
          One has not at all.                               1080
Thus it is, lady, whatever anyone might say,
With my lady, who changes and varies,
Gives and takes back, now hates, now is a beloved,
          And not in one place
Is all her heart, and if anyone shares in it,             1085
Certainly I believe he has a poor share,
And that from him that share will soon disappear.
          No one could rightly consider
That a lover could hold another man so dear
That he would want him to share                           1090
In his loving, without more--that's not to be believed.
          And therefore completely
I cannot have her heart, so I lament it;
For a heart that in this way goes from hand to hand,
If a man possesses it at night, by morning he doesn't.  1095
          And in any case
The true lover is the proper bird of prey,
Since he, for any joy, wishes nothing
But the woman's heart which grants itself.
          So that I say                                    1100
That sooner you'll have your lover back
Than will her heart have so been changed
That it will be placed in me completely
          Never to be taken back;
For no man can remove the wolf's pelt                     1105
Without flaying him, nor can anyone make
A sparrow from a steer, or vice versa.
          And, sweet lady,
The custom is universal among men and women
That, when the soul has left the body,                    1110
And the body's in the ground beneath the stone,
          In a short time
It is forgotten, though one weeps for it.
For no man or woman whom I've ever seen has stayed
So long in sorrow never again to seek joy,               1115
          As soon as a year
Has passed, however loyal the lover,
And I won't except those of high or low degree.
And truly, I believe this is reasonable.
          So in this you'll follow                         1120
The custom; in no way will you break it.

Car ja de nul reprise n'en serez,
Et de bon cuer pour l'ame prierez.
        Mais en oubli
Ne puis mettre celle que pas n'oubli,        1125
Car Souvenir la tient moult près de mi
Sans departir jour, heure, ne demi;
        Et si la voy
Assez souvent, dont tous vis me desvoy,
Quant longuement de mes yeus la convoy,     1130
Et je n'en ay joie, ne bien, n'avoy;
        Eins voy autrui
Qui joie en a. C'est ce dont me destrui;
Car s'elle amer no vosist moy ne lui,
Les maus que j'ay ne pleingnisse a nelui,    1135
        Eins les portasse
Dedens mon cuer humblement et celasse,
Et en espoir de joie demourasse,
Si que meschief ne doleur ne doubtasse.
        Ne departir             1140
N'en vueil mon cuer, pour doubte dou partir,
Qui trop demeure en vie, et, sans mentir,
Je ne saroie amer a repentir.
        Et si seroie
Faus amoureus, se je me'en departoie,      1145
Car sans nul si li donnay l'amour moie.
Si l'ameray, que qu'avenir m'en doie;
        Et, par ma foy,
Si loiaument l'aim que j'ay plus d'anoy
Cent fois pour li que je n'aie pour moy,     1150
Quant s'onneur voy amenrir; car au doy
        La mousterront
Ceuls et celles qui cest ouevre saront,
Et meins assez en tous cas la croiront,      [16v]
Qu'a tous jours mais pour fausse la tenront.   1155
        Car de meffait
C'est un vice si villain et si lait,
Car qui le fait, ja de pooir qu'il ait,
N'iert de tous poins effacié ne deffait.
        Pour ce conclus,          1160
Dame, que j'ay de doleur assez plus,
Et que plus tost a garison venus
Seroit vos maus que cils dont sui tenus.
        Et jugement
En oseroie attendre vraiement,         1165
Se nous aviens juge qui loiaument
Vosist jugier, et veritablement."
        "Par m'ame, sire,


1145. EKJP repentoie--1150. MCBDEKJ Dis

For by none will you be scorned,
And with good heart you'll pray for the soul.
                    But I cannot
Forget her whom I have not forgotten,                         1125
Since Memory keeps her very close to me
Without leaving a day, an hour, not even half an hour;
                    And so I see her
Rather often, and this immediately undoes me,
When with my eyes I escort her a long time                    1130
Yet have no joy, no good, no guidance from it.
                    Instead I see another
Who has joy in it.  It's this that troubles me;
For if she didn't wish to love either me or him,
The pains that I have I would complain of to no one;          1135
                    Instead I'd bear them
Humbly within my heart and hide them,
And in hope of joy I would endure,
So that I'd fear neither misadventure nor pain.
                    And I don't wish                          1140
To take back my heart, for fear of desertion,
I who remain too long alive, and, it's no lie,
I do not know how to repent of loving.
                    And so I'd be
A false lover, if I left her,                                 1145
Since with no 'but' I gave her my love.
And I will love her, whatever I must come to in this;
                    And, by my faith,
I love her so loyally that I have a hundred times
More grief for her, than I have for me,                       1150
Since I see her honor ruined; for with their finger
                    They'll point her out,
Those men and women who know this business,
And much less they'll trust her in everything,
Since always they'll consider her false.                      1155
                    For in regard to dissemblance,
It's a vice so lowly and so ugly
That he who practices it, however powerful he may be,
Will never be completely rid of it, or reformed.
                    And so I conclude,                        1160
Lady, that I have much more pain,
And that sooner your ill will come
To cure than that by which I am held.
                    And the judgment
I would dare truly to expect,                                 1165
If we had a judge who faithfully
Would judge, and according to the truth."
                    "By my soul, sir,

Et de ma part je vueil et ose dire
Que de mon cuer le jugement desire.                                    1170
Or regardons qui nous volons eslire:
          Qui sans deport
Sache jugier li quels de nous a tort;
Car avis m'est que li maus que je port
Est si crueus qu'on ne puet plus sans mort."                           1175
          "Dame, je vueil
Que li juges soit fais tout a vo vueil."
"Mais au vostre, biau sire, et si conseil
Qu'il ne soit fais fors par vostre conseil,
          Car vous l'avez                                              1180
Premiers requis; pour ce dire devez."
"Certes, dame, or ne vous en lavez,
Mais vous, dites, pour ce que plus savez
          Que je ne fais."
Et quant je vi qu'il voloient que fais                                 1185
Fust jugemens de leurs dolereus fais,
Mes cuers en fu de joie tous refais.
          Si ne savoie
De deus choses la quele je feroie,
D'aler vers eaus, ou se je m'en tenroie.                               1190
Car volentiers mis les eüsse en voie
          De juge prendre
Tel qu'a jugier leurs fais peüst entendre,
Si souffissant qu'il n'i eüst qu'aprendre,*
Et qu'après lui n'i eüst que reprendre.                                1195
          Si m'avisay
Moult longuement, et pris mon avis ay
Que j'iroie a eaus. Lors sans delay
Je me levay et devers eaus alay
          Tout le couvert                                             1200
Parmi l'erbe qui estoit drue et vert;
Et quant je vins si près d'eaus qu'en apert
Les pos vëoir et tout a descouvert,
          Le petit chien
Prist a glatir qui ne me congnut rien,                                1205
Dont la dame qui moult savoit de bien
En tressailli (je m'en aperçu bien),
          Si l'apella.
Mais moult petit prisié son apel a,
Qu'en abaiant li chiennès m'aprocha,                                   1210
Tant que ses dens a ma robe acrocha.
          Si le hapay,
Dont il laissa de paour son abay.
Mais en mon cuer forment m'en deportay,
Pour ce qu'a sa dame le reportay,                                      1215

1171. EKJP regardez--1181. CDEKJP Premier

52

For my part I wish and dare to say
That with my heart I desire a judgment.                    1170
Now let's see whom we wish to choose:
          A man who without foolishness
Could determine which one of us is wrong;
For it seems to me that the troubles I bear are so cruel
That no one, this side of death, could have more."         1175
          "Lady, I wish
The judge to be whomever you desire."
"I yield to you, fair sir, and so I advise
That he be chosen only by your advice,
          For you have                                      1180
First sought him; therefore you must speak."
"Surely, my lady, you will not wash your hands of this now,
But please speak, since you know much more
          Than do I."
And when I saw that they wished                            1185
A judgment of their painful cases,
My heart was for this all changed to joy.
          And I did not know
Which of two things I would do:
Move toward them, or hold myself back.                     1190
For willingly I would have put them on the path
          Of taking on a judge
Who could undertake to judge their cases
So ably that they'd have to heed him,
Since, beside him, all others must be deemed inadequate.
          So I considered
For a long time, and decided that
I'd go to them.  Then without delay
I rose and went toward them
          Through all the brush                             1200
And through the grass which was so thick and green;
And when I had come so close to them that quite clearly
I could see them and without any hindrance,
          The little dog
Began to bark because he didn't know me at all,            1205
Because of which the lady who knew much of good
Startled (I saw this clearly),
          And so called him.
But he valued her calling hardly at all,
Since, barking, the dog approached me,                     1210
And finally tore at my robe with his teeth.
          Then I grabbed him,
And from fear he stopped his barking.
But in my heart I enjoyed this very much,
Because I returned him to his lady,                        1215

```
                Pour avoir voie
Et occoison d'aler ou je voloie;
Si que toudis son poil aplanioie,
Mais quant je vins ou estre desiroie,
                Je ne fui mie                           1220
Mus, n'esbahis; einsois a chiere lie
Ay salué toute la compaingnie,
Si com faire le sos de ma partie.
                Li chevaliers
Qui sages fu, courtois, et biaus parliers,        1225
Grans, lons, et drois, biaus, et gens, et legiers,  [17r]
Et d'onneur faire apris et coustumiers,
                Sans plus atendre
Courtoisement me vint mon salut rendre.
Et la dame ou Nature volt entendre                1230
Si qu'on ne puet sa grant biauté comprendre
                Vers moy se trait
Moult humblement, doucement, et a trait.*
Car elle avoit moult gracieus attrait
Et le maintien humble, dous, et parfait;          1235
                Et cheveus blons,
Les yex rians, plus vairs que nuls faucons,
Et ses corps fu gens, joins, gentils, et lons,
Et plus apers que nuls esmerillons;
                Et s'ot l'entrueil                      1240
Grandet a point, maniere et dous acueil,
Mais son attrait et son gent appareil
Qui simples fu n'avoit point de pareil;
                Et si fu blanche
Plus que la noif, quant elle est sus la branche,  1245
Sage, loial, courtoise, et de cuer franche,
Et si parfaite en toute contenance
                Qu'en loiauté
Estoit assez plus bele que biauté;
N'en li n'avoit orgueil, ne cruauté,              1250
Ne riens qui fust contraire a amité.
                Mais esplourée
Fu moult forment sa face coulourée;
Et nompourquant de coulour esmerée
Et de fine douçour estoit parée.                  1255
                Si m'apella
La dame, et puis m'enquist, et aparla
Moult sagement dont je venoie la.
Et je qui fui desirans d'oïr la,
                La verité                               1260
De chief en chief li ay dit et compté,
Comment la vins et ou j'avoie esté,
```

1232. A traist--1233. MCBDEKJP Moult bellement: all MSS attrait--
1242. EKJPR atour--1261. F conte

                To have the chance
And occasion to go where I wished;
And so all the time I stroked his fur,
But when I had come where I wanted to be,
                I was not at all                          1220
Ruffled or embarrassed; instead with a cheerful face
I saluted all the company,
As for my own part I knew how to do.
                The knight,
Who was wise, courteous, and well-spoken,            1225
Big, tall, and straight, handsome, and noble, and graceful,
Well-taught and accustomed to do the honorable thing,
                Without waiting longer
Courteously advanced to return my greeting.
And the lady in whom Nature wished to signify        1230
That no man could comprehend her overwhelming beauty
                Drew toward me
Quite serenely, softly, and slowly.
For she had a very gracious appearance
And her carriage was meek, sweet, and beyond reproach; 1235
                And her hair was blond,
Her eyes smiling, greyer than any falcon,
And her body was noble, well-shaped, pleasing, and long,
Better in form than any hunting bird:
                And the space between her eyes         1240
Was pleasantly wide, her manner and bearing sweet,
But her dress and her noble apparel,
Though simple, were beyond compare.
                She was whiter
Than the snow when it's on the bough,                1245
Wise, loyal, courteous, her heart generous,
And so perfect in every way
                That in her loyalty
She was much more beautiful than beauty itself.
There was in her neither haughtiness nor cruelty,   1250
Not anything that was contrary to friendship.
                Yet stained by tears
Was her face, much discolored;
And nonetheless she was endowed
With a pure complexion, with a refined sweetness.    1255
                And so the lady
Beckoned me, then questioned me, and spoke
Very wisely about whence I had come to that place.
And I who was desirous to hear her,
                Related and told                       1260
Her the truth of it from beginning to end,
How I had come there and where I had been,

En tant qu'il ont leur meschief raconté.
          Lors dist en bas
Li chevaliers par maniere de gas:*                    1265
"Je croy qu'il ait oÿ tous nos debas."
Et je li dis: "Sire, n'en doubtez pas,
          Que voirement
Les ay j'oïs moult ententivement
Et volentiers; mais n'aiez pensement                  1270
Que j'y pense fors bien; car vraiement
          Venus estoie
Sus un ruissel, par une herbue voie,
En ce vergier ou je me delitoie
Es oisillons que chanter escoutoie.                   1275
          Et quant einsi
Y fui venus, sire, je vous choisi,
Et d'autre part ma dame venir vi.
Si vous diray, comment je me chevi:
          Je regarday                                 1280
Le plus fueillu dou brueil; si m'i boutay,
Car de vous faire anui moult me doubtay;
Et la vos biens et vos maus escoutay
          De chief en chief.
Or m'est avis que de vostre meschief,                 1285
Et ma dame qui tient enclin son chief
Dou sien, sauriez volentiers le plus grief
          Par jugement.
Si ne volez penre premierement
Vostre juge, ne ma dame ensement.                     1290
Pour ce venus sui aviséement,
          Pour vous nommer
.I. chevalier qui moult fait a amer;*
Car de ça mer n'a pas, ne de la mer,
Plus gentil cuer, plus franc, n'a meins d'amer;       1295
          Car de largesse
Passe Alixandre et Hector de prouesse.
C'est li estos de toute gentillesse,
N'il ne vit pas com sers a sa richesse;
          Eins ne vuet rien                           1300
Fors que l'onneur de tout le bien terrien,
Et s'est plus liés, quant il puet dire: "Tien,"
Qu'uns couvoiteus n'est de penre dou sien.
          Dieu et l'eglise
Et loyauté aimme, et si bien justise                  1305
Qu'on le claimme l'Espée de Justise.
Humbles et dous est, et pleins de franchise
          A ses amis,                              [17v]
Fiers et crueus contre ses anemis.


1265-6. These lines are reversed in A--1287. F sariez

While they were recounting their misadventures.
                    Then the knight spoke
Softly, in a joking way:                                          1265
"I think he's heard all our debate."
And I said to him: "Sir, of this have no doubt at all,
            For truly
I have listened to it most attentively
And willingly; but you mustn't think                             1270
That I intend anything but good; for truly
            I came here
From above the stream, by a grassy path,
Into this orchard where I disported myself
With the birds whose song I listened to.                         1275
            And when in this way
I had come there, sir, I spotted you.
And on the other side I saw my lady come.
So I'll tell you how I provided for myself.
            I looked for                                          1280
The leafiest part of the greenery and pushed myself in,
Since I greatly feared I would annoy you;
And there I listened to your joys and sufferings
            From beginning to end.
Now it seems to me that you would                                1285
Willingly know which is the more grievous,
Your mischance, or that of the lady who holds her head down,
            Through a judgment.
You don't wish to be the first to
Select a judge, and neither does my lady.                        1290
So, under advisement, I came forward here
            To name for you
A knight who does much for love's sake;
For on this side of the sea or on the other
There is no heart nobler, none more generous, none less cruel;
            Since in generosity
He surpasses Alexander, and Hector in prowess.
He's the pillar of all nobility,
Nor does he live as a slave to his wealth.
            Instead he wants nothing                              1300
Except the honor of every worldly good,
And he's the happier, when he can say: "It's yours,"
Than the covetous man is to take from his goods.
            He loves God,
The church, and loyalty, and justice so much                     1305
That he's called the Sword of Justice.
He's humble and pleasant, full of generosity
            Toward his friends,
Fierce and cruel against his enemies.

Et, a briés mos, de scens, d'onneur, de pris                    1310
En porte adès au dit des bons le pris,
   Quel part qu'il veingne.
Et s'il avient que son anemi teingne
A son dessous, Nature li enseingne,
Et ses bons cuers, que pité li en prengne.                      1315
   C'est noble sorte,
Car Prouesse partout s'espée porte,
Hardiesse le conduit et enorte,
Et Largesse si li ouevre la porte
   De tous les cuers.                            1320
A ceaus qui sont bon (je n'en met nuls fuers),
Avec euls est com sont freres et suers,
Grans et petis, moiens, et a tous fuers.
   Sire, et d'Amours
Congnoist il tous les assaus, les estours,                      1325
Les biens, les maus, les plaintes, et les plours *
Miex qu'Ovides qui en sot tous les tours.
   Et se son nom,
Qui tant est bons et de noble renom,
Volez savoir, dites le moy, ou non."                            1330
"Certes, amis, dou savoir vous prion,
   Car onques mais,
Si come je croy, ne fu, ne n'iert jamais
Homme qui fust en tous cas si parfais,
Comme cils est, et par dis et par fais."                        1335
   "Sire, s'enseingne
Crie Lembourc, et est roys de Behaingne,
Fils de Henry, le bon roy d'Alemaingne,
Qui par force d'armes, qui que s'en plaingne,
   Comme emperere                               1340
Fu couronnez a Romme avec sa mere.
Dont s'il est bons, c'est bien drois qu'il appere:
Car il le doit et de mere et de pere.*
   Si que, biau sire,
Un tels juges seroit bons a eslire                              1345
Qui vous saroit bien moustrer et descrire
Li quels de vous sueffre plus de martire:
   Si le prenez."
Li chevaliers respondi com senez:
"Je croy que Diex nous ait ci amenez."                          1350
Et dist: "Dame, s'a juge le tenez,
   Je m'i ottroy."
Et la dame respondi sans desroy:
"Sire, tant oy dire de bien dou roy,
Tant est sages, preus, et de bon arroy                          1355
   Que je l'acort."


1322. CEKJ Auec iui--1326. A plaites--1342. CEKJP cest raison-
1343. A doit de; FCDEKJ pere et de mere

58

And, in a few words, for intelligence, honor, and worth
He always takes the prize, as good men say,
   Wherever he may go.
And if it happens that he gets the upper hand
Over his enemy, Nature teaches him,
And his own good heart, that he should take pity on him.
   He's a noble example,
For Prowess everywhere bears his sword,
Hardihood escorts him, encourages him,
And Generosity opens for him the door
   Of every heart.       1320
To those who are good (I make no exceptions),
To them he is like a brother and sister,
To the great and small, those in between, and in every way.
   Sir, of Love
He knows all the assaults, the skirmishes,   1325
The joys, the pains, the sorrowing and moaning
Better than Ovid himself, who knew all its doings.
   And if his name,
Which is so good and of such gentle renown,
You wish to know, tell me yes or no."   1330
"Why yes, my friend, we beg you to tell us,
   For never yet,
If it is who I think, has any man ever been,
Nor no man ever was in all ways so perfect
As this man is, in both word and deed."   1335
   "Sir, his flag
Cries out Luxembourg, and he is King of Bohemia,
Son to Henry, the good King of Germany,
Who by force of arms, whoever might bemoan it,
   As Emperor       1340
Was crowned at Rome with his mother.
So if he's good, it's certainly right that he seem so,
For he owes it to his mother and his father.
   And so, fair sir,
It would be wise to pick such a judge,   1345
One who could skillfully demonstrate and decide
Which of you suffers the greater pain:
   So choose him."
The knight responded like a wise man:
"I believe that God has led us here."   1350
And he said: "Madam, if you take him for our judge,
   I will agree to it."
And the lady answered without any foolishness:
"Sir, I have heard so much good spoken of this king,
Who is so wise, so brave, of such fine following,   1355
   That 1 concur."

"Grant merci, dame; or sommes en acort.
Si pri a Dieu que le bon roy confort
Et qu'il nous maint temprement a bon port,
   Si que parler      1360
Puissiens a lui, ou il nous faut aler."
Je respondi: "Bien vous say assener
La ou il est et, s'il vous plaist, mener.
   Certeins en  sui,
Car vraiement, je mengay yer et bui   1365
Avec sens gens en chastiau de Durbui.*
Et il y est, ne n'en partira hui;
   Ne ce n'est mie
Loing, qu'il n'i a ne lieue ne demie,
Nom pas de ci le quart d'une huchie."  1370
Li chevaliers d'aler la dame en prie
   Sans plus atendre.
La dame dist: "Je ne m'en quier deffendre,
Mais je ne say quel part la voie prendre."
Je dis: "Dame, bien le vous vueil aprendre. 1375
   Venez adès.
J'iray devant et vous venrez après."
Si qu'en chemin me mis, d'aler engrès.
Et quant il ont veü Durbui de près,
   Si s'arrestoient,      1380
Et dou veoir forment se mervilloient,
Car onques mais en leur vie n'avoient
Veü si bel, ne si gent, ce disoient.
   Et, sans doubtance,
Il est moult fors et de trés grant plaisance, 1385
Biaus et jolis et de po de deffence.
Car se li rois d'Alemaingne et de France
   Devant estoient,
Cil de dedens ja pour ce ne lairoient
Qu'il n'alassent hors et ens, s'il voloient, [18r] 1390
Toutes les fois qu'a besongnier aroient
   En la contrée.
C'est une roche en mi une valée
Qui tout entour est d'iaue environnée,
Grande, bruiant, parfonde, roide, et lée;  1395
   Et li vergier
Sont tout entour si bel qu'a droit jugier,
On ne porroit nuls plus biaus souhaidier.
Mais d'oisillons y a si grant frapier
   Que jour et nuit      1400
La valée retentist de leur bruit;
Et l'iaue aussi seriement y bruit,
Si qu'on ne puet en nul milleur deduit.


1378. F quau

60

"Many thanks, lady; now we are agreed.
And I pray that God may comfort the good king
And that He may lead us safely to good harbor,
      So that we                          1360
Might speak to him, wherever we must go."
I answered: "I know myself how to tell you quite well
Where he is, and, if you please, to lead you there.
      I am certain of it,
For it is true that I ate and drank yesterday      1365
With his court in Durbuy Castle.
He's still there; he will not leave today;
      Nor is it
Very far from here, not even a league, or half a league,
Not the quarter of the distance a voice will carry."    1370
The knight then asked the lady to set out
      Without waiting any longer.
The lady said: "I don't want to refuse,
But I do not know which path to take."
I said: "Lady, I wish very much to show you.      1375
      Proceed now.
I'll go ahead and you will follow after."
And so I started out, eager to go.
And when they saw Durbuy Castle close by,
      They stopped                     1380
And greatly marvelled in looking it over,
Since never before in their lives had they
Seen any place so beautiful, so noble, or so they said.
      And, no doubt,
It is a very secure and attractive spot,      1385
Beautiful and pleasing, in little need of defense.
For if the kings of both Germany and France
      Were before it,
Those inside would never need to give up
Exiting and entering, if they wished,      1390
At any time that they had need to travel
      Into the surrounding country.
It's an elevation in the middle of a valley,
Which is thoroughly encompassed by a river
That's huge, noisy, deep, rough, and wide:      1395
      And the woods
All around are so pretty that, to judge correctly,
None prettier could ever be hoped for.
In them, however, is such a huge crowd of birds
      That night and day                 1400
The valley resounds with their singing.
And the river also makes a loud noise,
So that one can find no greater joy.

```
            Et puis après
A grans roches tout entour, nom pas près,                    1405
Eins sont si loing dou chastel qu'il n'est fers,
Engiens, ne ars qui y getast james.
            Mais la maison
Sus la roche est si bien qu'onques mais hom
Ne vit autre de plus belle façon,                            1410
Car il n'y a nesune meffaçon.
            Et la fonteinne
Est en la court, qui n'est mie villeinne;
Eins est vive, de roche clere et seinne,
Froide com glace et plus douce que Seinne.                   1415
            Mais le vaissel
Ou elle chiet est tailliez a cisel
D'un marbre fin, blanc, et bis, et si bel
Que tels ne fu depuis le temps Abel.
            Sus la riviere                                   1420
Est la prée large, longue, et pleniere,
Ou on trueve d'erbes mainte maniere.
Mais revenir m'estuet a ma matiere.
            Quant la maison
Orent veü, je les mis a raison,                              1425
Et si leur dis: "De l'aler est saison.
Alons nous en; car ci riens ne faison."
            Si en alames
Tout le chemin et le pont trespassames,
Ne ça ne la, nulle par n'arrestames                          1430
Jusques a tant qu'a la porte hurtames.
            Mais li portiers
La porte ouvri de cuer et volentiers
Je qui hurtay et qui fui li premiers
Et de laiens estre assez coustumiers                         1435
            Parlay einsi:
"Cils chevaliers et ceste dame aussi
Viennent parler au roy, s'il est yci."
Et li portiers tantost me respondi
            Qu'il y estoit.*                                 1440
Je dis: "Amis, pren garde, s'on porroit
Parler a li." Et il dist qu'il iroit.
Mais tout einsi com de nous se partoit
            Pour aler sus,
Uns chevaliers, biaus, et gens, et corsus,                   1445
Jolis et gais, en est a nous venus;
Honneur ot nom, et s'en sot plus que nuls.
            N'il ne vint mie
Tous seuls a nous; eins li fist compaingnie
Une dame belle, gaie, et jolie;                              1450
```

1421. CBDEKJ longe large--1435. CEKJP iere assez--1440. AC Qui

62

                    And then further
There are great cliffs all around, not too close,          1405
But rather they are so far from the castle that no iron,
No siege machine, no bow could ever be shot at it from there.
                    And the keep
Above the rocks is so well-made that never
Did any man see another of more beautiful appearance,      1410
Since there's no defect at all.
                    And the spring
In the courtyard is not unpleasant at all;
Instead it's free-flowing, from clean and healthy rock,
As cold as ice, sweeter than the Seine,                    1415
                    But the fountain
Into which it falls is shaped by chisels
From fine marble, white and grayish brown, and so pretty
That there's been none like it since Abel's time.
                    Above the river bank                    1420
The meadow's broad, long, and full,
Where one finds many kinds of plants.
But I must return to my matter.
                    When they had looked over
The residence, I gave them counsel                         1425
And said: "It's time to go.
Let us proceed; for here we're accomplishing nothing."
                    So we went down
The entire path and crossed the bridge,
Nor did we halt either here or there                       1430
Until finally we knocked upon the gate.
                    And the porter
Opened the gate cordially and willingly.
I who knocked and was in front
And was rather accustomed to being inside                  1435
                    Spoke thus:
"This knight and this lady as well
Have come to speak with the king, if he is here."
And the porter quickly answered me
                    That he was there.                      1440
I said: "Friend, please find out if one might
Speak to him." And he said that he would go.
But just as he was leaving us
                    To go above,
A knight, handsome, and noble, and broad-shouldered,       1445
Friendly and jolly, came toward us;
His name was Honor, and he knew more about it than anyone.
                    And in no way had he come
All alone to us; instead a beautiful lady,
Gay and friendly, was his companion                        1450

Si ot a nom la dame Courtoisie.
       Bien y parut,
Car aussi tost qu'elle nous aperçut
Nous salua, et puis biau nous reçut.
Si fist Honneur, si com faire le dut.        1455
       Adont andoy
Courtoisement, en riant, sans effroy,
Prirent chascun l'un d'eaus .ii. par le doy.
Mais Courtoisie, einsi com dire doy,
       Le chevalier        1460
Acompaingna liement, sans dangier,
Et Honneur volt la dame acompaingnier;
Lors se prirent ensamble a desraisnier.
       Si s'en alerent,
Tout en parlant, la ou il les menerent,        1465
Par les degrez de marbre qu'il monterent,
Tant qu'en la chambre au bon roy s'en entrerent.
       Et li bons rois,
Qui moult estoit sages en tous endrois,
Loiaus, vaillans, liberaus, et adrois,        1470
Et envers tous dous, humbles, et courtois,
       En moult grant joie
Estoit assis sur .i. tapis de soie,        *[18v]*
Et ot .i. clerc que nommer ne saroie
Qui li lisoit la bataille de Troie.        1475
       Mais Hardiesse
L'acompaingnoit, et sa fille Prouesse,
Et doucement tint par la main Largesse,
Une dame de moult grant gentillesse.
       S'i fu Richesse,        1480
Amour, Biauté, Loiauté, et Leësse,
Desirs, Pensers, Volenté, et Noblesse,
Franchise, Honneur, Courtoisie, Juenesse.
       Cil seize estoient
Avec le roy, n'onques ne s'en partoient.        1485
Diex et Nature ottroié li avoient,
Dès qu'il fu nez; pour ce tout le servoient.
       C'estoit grant grace.
Et s'il y a nul ne nulle qui face
Chose dont nuls puist dire qu'il mefface        1490
Raisons y est qui le meffait efface.
       Einsi se sist
Li gentils rois, et quant la dame vist,
Il se leva, et par la main la prist,
Car Courtoisie a faire li aprist.        1495
       Après pris a
Le chevalier, et forment l'esprisa

1456. A en doy--1458. F lun des--1488. A cestot--1493. F vit--
1497. CBDKJ le prisa

And she was called Lady Courtesy.
              And truly she seemed to be that,
For as soon as she spied us,
She greeted us, and then received us graciously.
Honor did the same, just as he should do.          1455
              And then those two
Courteously, while smiling, without ado,
Took each one of these two by the hand.
And Courtesy, as I ought to say,
              Accompanied                             1460
The knight gleefully, with no difficulty,
And Honor wished to accompany the lady;
Then they grouped themselves to go away.
              And so they left,
Talking the whole time, where they were led,        1465
Up some marble stairs that they mounted
Until they finally entered the good king's hall.
              And the good king,
Who was wise in every way,
Loyal, valiant, generous, and well-mannered,        1470
And toward everyone sweet, humble, and courteous,
              In very great contentment
Was seated on a silk rug,
And some clerk whom I cannot name
Was reading to him the battle of Troy.              1475
              And Hardihood
Accompanied him, and Prowess, his daughter, as well,
And he held Generosity quite softly by the hand,
A lady of very great nobility.
              And Wealth was there,                  1480
Love, Beauty, Loyalty, and Happiness,
Desire, Thought, Will, and Nobility,
Liberality, Honor, Courtesy, Youth.
              These sixteen were
With the king and never left his side;              1485
God and Nature had bestowed them on him
At his birth; and thus all served him.
              The gift was a great one.
And if any gentleman or lady ever did
Anything that could be called a misdeed,            1490
Reason was there to erase the fault.
              And thus the noble king
Was seated, and when he saw the lady,
He rose, and took her by the hand,
For Courtesy had taught him to do this.             1495
              Afterward he received
The knight, and carefully judged him

Dedens son cuer, et puis leur demanda
Moult sagement dont il venoient la,
   Et leur enquist          1500
De leur estre qui moult li abelist.
Li chevaliers a la dame requist
Qu'elle li vosist dire; et elle dist
   Que non feroit;
Einsois deïst, que miex li afferoit.       1505
Il respondi adont qu'il li diroit
De chief en chief tout einsi qu'il estoit,
   Jusqu'a la fin.
"Sire," dist il, "ci près a .i. jardin
Vert et flouri ou il a grant tintin      1510
De rossignols; s'i vins hui a matin,
   Pour escouter
Leur biau service et leur joli chanter,
Comment que po s'i peüst deporter
Mon cuer que riens ne porroit conforter.    1515
   Mais toute voie
Einsi venus d'aventure y estoie,
Pleins et pensis de maus qu'Amours m'envoie,
Si vi venir par une estroite voie
   Verde et herbue          1520
Ceste dame qu'avec moy est venue.
Si me sambla de maniere esperdue,
Si que tantost pris parmi l'erbe drue
   Mon adresse ay,
Et mon chemin droit vers li adressay.     1525
Et quant je fui près, je la saluay,
Mais mot ne dist, dont je me mervillay,
   Ne onques chiere
Ne fist de moy, ne d'oueil, ne de maniere.
Et je qui fui mervilleus pour quoy c'iere,   1530
Dis belement: "Trés douce dame chiere,
   Pour quel raison
Ne volez vous entendre a ma raison?
Et la tiray par le pan dou giron.
S'en tressailli, dont sa belle façon     1535
   Coulour mua.
Si respondi, que plus n'i arresta,
Et durement envers moy s'escusa      [19r]
De son penser a quoy elle musa.
   Et li enquis           1540
Pourquoy son cuer estoit einsi pensis.
Finablement tant parlay et tant fis
Qu'elle me dist tout ce que je li quis,
   Voire par si

1524. EKJ Men adrecay--1538. DEKJ doucement

In his heart, and then asked them
Wisely why they had come,
      And inquired about 1500
Their station, which pleased him greatly.
The knight asked the lady
If she would speak to the king; and she said
      That she would not do it;
Instead he should speak, since this would impress him more.
He answered then that he would tell him
Everything step by step, just how it stood,
      Until the end.
"Sire," he said, "close by is a garden
Green and flowery where there's a great chorus 1510
Of nightingales; and so I went there this morning
      To listen to
Their beautiful service and their pleasant singing,
Even though my heart could find there
Little pleasure, for nothing can comfort it. 1515
      But immediately
When I had come there by chance,
Full of the pains Love sends me and thinking on them,
I saw arrive by a narrow path,
      Green and grassy, 1520
This lady who's come here with me.
And her manner seemed to me distraught,
So that at once through the lush grass,
      I made my way,
And directed my steps right toward her. 1525
And when I was close, I greeted her,
But she didn't say a word; therefore I wondered,
      And she didn't take
Notice of me, not with her eye, nor with her manner.
And I who was bewildered why this was so, 1530
Said pleasantly: "Very sweet dear lady,
      For what reason
Do you wish not to heed my speech?
And I tugged at the hem of her robe.
And she startled at this, so that her pretty face 1535
      Changed color.
Then she responded without a pause,
And fervently apologized to me
For the thought at which she was musing.
      And I asked her 1540
Why her heart was so pensive.
At last I had said and done so much
That she told me what I asked her,
      So truthfully

Que par ma foy li juray et plevi,                          1545
Quant elle aroit son parler assevi,
Que le penser li diroie de mi.
   Et dist einsi
Q'elle soloit avoir loial ami
Qui loiaument l'amoit, et elle li.                         1550
Mais la mort l'a de ce siecle parti,
   Et la valour,
Le sens, le pris, la prouesse, l'onnour,
Qui fu en li, si comme elle dist, flour,
Le fist estre des bons tout le millour.                    1555
   Pour ce pensoit
Parfondement, ne onques ne cessoit,
Et en pensant le plouroit et plaingnoit,
Si que son vis en larmes se baingnoit.
   Pour ce maintient                          1560
Que la dolour est plus griés qui li vient
Pour son amy que celle qui me tient.
Sire, et je di, faire le me couvient,
   Tout le contraire.
J'aim loyaument de cuer et sans retraire                   1565
La plus trés bele et le plus dous viaire
Qu'onques encor Nature peüst faire,
   Qui me donna
Jadis son cuer tout et abandonna.
Son cuer, s'amour, son amy me clama                        1570
Et par son dit seur tous autres m'ama.
   Or est einsi,
Sire, qu'elle n'a mais cure de my;
Eins m'a guerpi, et fait nouvel amy.
Et, par m'ame, pas ne l'ay desservi.                       1575
   Et d'autre part,
Mon guerredon ailleurs donne et depart,
Ne je n'en puis avoir ne part ne hart:
C'est ce, sire, pour quoy li cuers me part.
   Si m'est avis,                             1580
Consideré mes raisons, que j'ay pis
Que la dame, comment que ses amis
Soit trespassez, Diex l'ait en paradis!
   Sire, et cils clers
Qui me samble gais, jolis, et apers,                       1585
Fu atapis ou jardin et couvers
En plus espès dou brueil qui est tous vers.
   Si sailli hors,
Quant li ot bien oÿ tous nos descors.
Si nous loa que li drois et li tors                        1590
Fust mis seur vous, et ce fu nos acors.


1555. F estres des bons

That on my faith I swore and pledged to her                    1545
That when she had concluded her speech,
I would tell her my own thought.
        And so she said
That once she had a faithful lover,
Who loved her loyally, and she him.                            1550
But death took him from this world,
        And the valor,
The intelligence, the worth, the prowess, the honor,
Which, as she said, had in him their flower,
Had made him among good men the very best.                     1555
        For this reason she thought
Deeply, nor ever did she cease,
And, while thinking, cried for and bemoaned him,
So that her face was bathed in tears.
        And so she maintains                1560
That the pain is more grievous which comes to her
For her lover's sake than that which holds me.
Sire, and I say, it is necessary that I do so,
        Just the contrary.
I love loyally from the heart, without desisting,             1565
The most beautiful and the sweetest form
That ever yet Nature has been able to create,
        Who gave me
Once her heart completely and abandoned it.
Her heart, her love, her lover she called me,                 1570
And so she said she loved me above all others.
        Now it is thus,
Sire, namely that she no  longer cares about me;
Instead, she's thrown me over, and taken a new lover.
And, by my soul, I haven't deserved this at all.              1575
        And elsewhere
She gives and shares what was my reward,
Nor of this can I have either share or part.
For this reason, Sire, my heart deserts me.
        So it seems,                        1580
Considering my reasons, that I have it worse
Than the lady, since, although her lover
Has passed away, God has him in paradise!
        Sire, and this clerk
Who seems friendly and merry  and knowledgeable               1585
Was hidden in the greenery and covered up
In the thickest part of the brush which is all green.
        So he emerged,
After he had clearly heard all our argument.
And he advised us to put the right and wrong of it            1590
To you, and this was our bargain.

```
          Car longuement
Avoit duré de nous le parlement,
Et si aviens fait meint arguement,
Si comme il est escript plus pleinnement            1595
          Ici dessus.
Or sommes ci par devers vous venus,
Par quoy li drois soit jugiez et sceüs,
Et que vos dis soit de nous .ii. tenus.
          Si que ce plait                           1600
Povez tantost terminer, s'il vous plaist;
Car nous avons de vous no juge fait.
Sire, or avez oÿ tout nostre fait
          Entierement;
Si en vueilliez faire le jugement,                  1605
Car nous l'avons desiré longuement,
Et ceste dame et moy devotement
          Vous en prions."


Quant cils li ot moustreés leurs raisons,
Qui bien le sot faire com sages homs,               1610
Li gentils rois qui moult estoit preudons
          Li respondi:
"Se Diex me gart, vous avez pris en my
Juge ignorant et de sens  desgarni,
Ne onques mais je n'oÿ, ne ne vi                    1615
          Tel jugement;
S'en saroie jugier petitement.
Mais nompourquant le conseil de ma gent
En vueil avoir; car je l'ay bel et gent."
          Lors appella                   [19v] 1620
En sousriant Loiauté qui fu la,
Amour, Juenesse, et Raison, qui parla
Premierement, et puis leur demanda
          Li gentils roys:
"Que diriez vous qui savez tous les drois?          1625
Cils chevaliers qui gens est et adrois
Et ceste dame aussi a ces crins blois
          Sont venu ci
Par devers moy, dont je les remercy,
Et jugement vuelent oïr de my,                       1630
Li quels a plus de mal et de sousci:
          La dame avoit
Ami loial qui l'amoit et servoit,
Et elle lui, tant comme elle pooit.
Or est einsi que Mors, qui tout reçoit,             1635
          Li a tollu.
S'en a le cuer dolent et irascu,
```

1625. CDEKJP dittes

```
              For our discussion
Had lasted a long time,
And we had made many arguments,
Just as it is written more fully                        1595
              Here above.
Now we have come here before you,
So that the right may be judged and known,
And that your sentence may be kept by us two.
              And so this debate                        1600
You can end at once, if it pleases you;
For we have made you our judge.
Sire, now you have heard all our doings
              In full;
So please make the decision in this,                    1605
Since we've desired one a long time,
And this lady and I earnestly
              Beg you for it."

When he had put their cases to him,
This man who knew well how to do so wisely,             1610
The noble king who was a very worthy man,
              Answered him:
"So God keep me, you have chosen in me
A judge ignorant and lacking in discernment,
For never before have I heard or seen                   1615
              Such a case;
And little I know about judging it.
But nonetheless I would like to hear the counsel
Of my court in this; for I have one both noble and good."
              Then he called,                           1620
As he smiled, Loyalty, who was there,
Love, Youth, and Reason, who spoke
First, and then the noble king
              Asked them:
"What would you say, who know all the laws?             1625
This knight who is noble and well-mannered
And also this lady with the blonde hair
              Have come here
Before me, for which I thank them,
And wish to hear a judgment from me,                    1630
Namely which of them suffers greater pain and care.
              The lady had
A loyal lover who loved and served her,
And she him, as much as she could.
Now it happens that Death, who receives everyone,      1635
              Has taken him from her.
Therefore her heart is sorrowful and troubled,
```

Car a son temps ot il si grant vertu
Que nul milleur, ne nul plus bel ne fu.
                    Le chevalier
Sans repentir aimme de cuer entier
La plus bele qui vive, a son cuidier,
Et elle foy sans muer, ne changier
                    Li a promis,
Et retenus fu de li comme amis
Et bien amez; il en estoit tous fis.
Or a la dame en autre son cuer mis,
                    Et li guerpi
Dou tout en tout, et n'a cure de li.
Et a ses yex voit la belle et celi
Qui les dous biens a qu'il a desservi.
                    Or vous ay dit
Pour quoy il sont venu oïr mon dit.
Et sans doubte, cuers qui einsi languit
Se destruit moult, et a grant doleur vit.
                    Si m'en devez
Donner conseil au mieux que vous poez;
Car chascuns est mes drus et mes privez,
Et moult me fi en vous, bien le savez.
                    Dites, Raison.
Premiers oïr vueil vostre entention;
Car vous m'avez maint conseil donné bon."
Raisons, qui fu bele et de bon renom,
                    Einsi respont:
"Sire, je di que cil .ij. amant sont
Moult engoisseus, quant einsi perdu ont
Ce qu'il aimment, et que li cuers leur font,
                    Si com la cire
Devant le feu se degaste et empire.
Mais qu'il soient tuit pareil de martire
Et de meschief, ce ne vueil je pas dire.
                    Ce qui me muet
Vous vueil dire, puisque faire l'estuet:
Ceste dame jamais veoïr ne puet
Son ami vray, einsi comme elle suet.
                    Si avenra
Einsi que, puisque plus ne le verra,
Je feray tant qu'elle l'oubliera,
Car le cuers ja tant chose n'amera
                    Qu'il ne l'oublie
Par eslongier. Certes, je ne di mie
Qu'une piece n'en ait peinne et hachie,
Mais Juenesse qui tant est gaie et lie
                    Ne soufferroit


1665. AFMBD amans

For in his time he had such great virtue
That there was none better, none more handsome.
      The knight,                    1640
Without repenting of it, loves with his whole heart
The most beautiful woman alive, according to his judgment,
And she has pledged her faith to him not to alter,
      Not to change,
And he was accepted by her as her lover        1645
And well loved; he was quite certain of it.
Now the lady has given her heart to another man,
      And thrown him over
Completely in everything, and has no concern for him.
And with his eyes he sees the beautiful lady and the man
Who possesses the sweet goods he has deserved.
      Now I've told you
Why they have come to hear my sentence.
And, without doubt, a heart that languishes so
Greatly destroys itself, and lives in much pain.      1655
      So in this you ought
To render me counsel, the best you can;
For each of you is my intimate and friend,
And I trust very much in you, as well you know.
      Speak, Reason.             1660
First I would hear your opinion;
For you have given me much good advice."
Reason, who was beautiful and of good repute,
      Answered in this way:
"Sire, I say that these two lovers are         1665
Greatly anguished, because they've in this way lost
Those whom they love, and also that their hearts are failing,
      Just as the wax
Before the flame wastes away, grows smaller.
But that they are exactly equal in suffering     1670
And misfortune, this I don't wish to say.
      What sways me
I'll state, since it is necessary to do so:
This lady can never see
Her true lover, as she was wont to do.        1675
      And so it will happen
Thus that, since she will no longer see him,
I'll work in such a way that she'll forget him,
For the heart will never love a thing so much
      That it'll not forget it         1680
As time goes by. Of course, I don't say at all
That for a while she won't have pain and torment,
But Youth,who is so very gay and happy,
      Will not allow

Pour nulle riens qu'entroubliez ne soit.                    1685
Car Juenesse, sire, comment qu'il voit,
Met en oubli moult tost ce que ne voit.
      Après je di
Qu'Amours n'a pas tant de pooir en li
Que soustenir se peüst sans amy                             1690
L'eure d'un jour, ne sans amie aussi.*
      Et se l'un faut
Des .iij., li .ij. autres aront deffaut;
Qu'Amours, ami, et amie estre faut
Tout ensamble, ou l'amour riens ne vaut.                    1695
      Et puisqu'amie
Et Amours ont perdu la compaingnie
D'ami, certes, je ne donroie mie
De leur amour une pomme porrie.
      C'est assavoir,                       1700
Quant a l'amour qui est mondeinne, avoir.
Car c'est trés bon de faire son devoir,                     [20r]
Si que l'ame s'en puist apercevoir.
      Mais il n'est ame,
N'homme vivant qui aimme si sans blame                      1705
S'il est tapez de l'amoureuse flame,
Qu'il n'aimme miex assez le corps que l'ame.
      Pour quel raison?
Amour vient de charnel affection,
Et si desir et sa condition                                 1710
Sont tuit enclin a delectation.
      Si ne se puet
Nuls, ne nulle garder qui amer vuet
Qu'il n'i ait vice ou pechié; il l'estuet,
Et c'est contraire a l'ame qui s'en duet.                   1715
      Et d'autre part,
Tout aussi tost com l'ame se depart
Dou corps, l'amour s'en eslonge et espart.
Einsi le voy partout, se Diex me gart.
      Si que l'amour                        1720
De ceste dame, ou tant a de valour,
Apetise toudis de jour en jour;
Et aussi fait a ce fuer la dolour.
      Mais cils amis
Qui folement s'est d'amer entremis                          1725
Sans mon conseil, et se s'i est si mis,
Li dolereus, qu'il en est tous remis,
      Les maus d'amer
Sont en son cuer qui li sont trop amer;
Qu'Amours le fait nuit et jour enflamer,                    1730
N'il ne vorroit, ne porroit oublier


1691. ACD du jour--1705. CEKJ Ne homs viuans

For any reason that he should not be forgotten.                    1685
For Youth, sire, although he sees,
Puts into oblivion very quickly what he doesn't see.
          I state further
That Love doesn't have enough power in it
That it can sustain itself without the lover                        1690
An hour of a day, nor without the beloved either.
          And if one is lacking
Of these three, the two others will fail;
For Love, lover, and beloved must remain
Together, or the love affair's worth nothing.                       1695
          And since beloved
And Love have lost the companionship
Of the lover, to be sure, I would not give
A rotten apple for their love affair.
          As far as love which is earthly                           1700
Is concerned, experiencing it is having it.
For it's very good in doing its job,
So that the soul can feel it.
          But there is no soul,
No living man who loves in this way without sin                     1705
If he is struck by the amorous flame,
So that he doesn't love the body much more than the soul.
          For what reason?
Love arises from a fleshly attraction,
And its desire and its nature                                       1710
Are completely inclined toward enjoyment.
          And so no man
And no woman who wishes to love can prevent
Vice or sin from being in it; it must be so,
And this is contrary to the soul which sorrows over it.
          And furthermore,
As soon as the soul departs
From the body, love leaves and distances itself.
This is exactly what I see everywhere, may God keep me.
          And so the love                                           1720
Of this lady, in which there is so much strength,
Diminishes constantly from day to day;
And her suffering does so also just the same way.
          But this lover
Who has madly undertaken to love                                    1725
Against my advice, and so has begun it,
This unfortunate one, who's all weakened by this,
          The pains of love
Which are in his heart are too bitter for him;
For Love makes him burn by night and day,                           1730
Nor would he, nor could he forget

75

                    Son annemie.
Savez pourquoy ?  Pour ce que Compaingnie,
Amour, Biauté, et Juenesse la lie,
Et Loiauté, qu'oublier ne vueil mie,                          1735
                    En grant folie,
En rage, en dueil, et en forcenerie
Le font languir, et en grant jalousie,
Et en peril de l'ame et de la vie.
                    Car main et tart                          1740
Son dolent cuer de sa dame ne part,
Eins la compaingne en tous lieus sans depart;*
Et cils qui est plus près dou feu, plus s'art.
                    Et Loiauté
Si li deffent a faire fausseté.                                1745
Mais s'il eüst par mon conseil ouvré
Quant sa dame ot nuef ami recouvré,
                    Il n'eüst pas
Continué l'amour; car, en tel cas,
Se la dame chante en haut ou en bas,                          1750
On doit aler ou le trot ou le pas.
                    Après li dist
Biauté qu'il fait miex assez, s'il languist,
Pour li amer, que se d'autre joïst.
Si fait Amour.  Juenesse le norrist                            1755
                    Avec folour
En ce meschief, en celle fole errour,
Car il en pert le sens et la vigour.
Einsi languist li dolens en dolour;
                    Car quant il voit                          1760
Que de s'amour, present li, autres joit,
Qui son amy appeler le soloit,
Il a le cuer si jalous, si destroit,
                    Que c'est merveille
Qu'il ne s'occist, ou qu'il ne s'apareille                    1765
D'occirre ce qui einsi le traveille;
Et ce li met jalousie en l'oreille.
                    Et s'il avoit
L'amour de li, einsi comme il soloit,
Qu'en feroit il ?  Certes, riens n'en feroit.                 1770
Car jamais jour il ne s'i fieroit.
                    Et pour c'espoir
N'a de jamais autre solas avoir,
Puisque mettre ne puet en nonchaloir
Ceste dame qui tant le fait doloir.                           1775
                    Si que je di
Qu'il a plus mal que ceste dame ci,
Et que son cuer est en plus grant sousci,


1742. AFMEKJ Eins le

                       76

                His enemy.
Do you know why?   Because Companionship,
Love, Beauty, and joyous Youth,
And Loyalty, whom he doesn't wish to forget,              1735
                Make him languish
In great madness, in rage,
In distraction, and in great jealousy,
And in the peril of his soul and life.
                For early and late                        1740
His sorrowing heart never leaves his lady,
But instead accompanies her everywhere without departing;
And he who is closer to the fire gets more burned.
                And Loyalty
Prevents him from proving false.                          1745
But if he had acted according to my advice
When his lady had found a new lover,
                He would not have
Continued the love affair; for, in such a case,
If the lady sings high or low,                            1750
The man must travel at a trot or a walk.
                Afterward Beauty
Told him he'd do much better, if he languished,
In loving her, than in taking joy from another.
Love did likewise.  Youth nourished him                   1755
                With madness
In this misfortune, in this crazy error,
So that because of it he lost strength and wit.
Thus the grieving man languished in grief;
                But when he sees                          1760
That another, with him present, rejoices in his beloved,
The lady who was accustomed to call him her lover,
His heart is so jealous, so distraught,
                That it's a wonder
He doesn't kill himself, or make ready                    1765
To kill the one who tortures him so.
And jealousy puts this in his ear.
                And if he had
Her love, just as he was accustomed to,
What would he do with it?   Surely, he'd do nothing.      1770
For never would he trust in it a single day.
                And therefore he has
No hope of ever having other comfort,
Since he cannot cool in his affections
For this lady who hurts him so much.                      1775
                And so I say
That he has more pain than this lady here,
And that his heart is in much greater anguish over it,

Par les raisons que vous avez oÿ.
    Et, a mon gré,          1780
Cils chevaliers en a moult bien parlé,
Car en escript l'ay ci dessus trouvé,
Et par raison s'entention prouvé.
     Ce m'est avis."        [20v]
Quant Raisons ot moustré tout son avis,    1785
Amours parla qui fu biaus a devis,
Et gracieus de maniere et de vis,
     Et dist: "Raison,
Moult bien avez moustrée vo raison.
Si m'i ottroy, fors tant que mesprison    1790
Feroit d'oster son cuer de la prison
     A la trés bele
Pour qui il sent l'amoureuse estincelle.
Si vueil qu'il l'aint et serve comme celle
Dont eü a mainte lie nouvelle,      1795
     Car s'il pooit
Vivre mil ans, et toudis la servoit,
Ja par servir il ne desserviroit
Les grans douceurs que faire li soloit.
     Et se Plaisance,       1800
Qui faire fait mainte estrange muance,
Li fait estre de sa dame en doubtance,
Doit il estre pour c'en desesperance?
     Certes, nanil!
Qu'en mon service en a encor cent mil    1805
Qui aimment tuit près aussi fort comme il,
Et si n'en ont la monte d'un fusil.
     Et s'ay povoir
De li garir et de li desdoloir,
Mais il n'a mais fiance, ne espoir,     1810
En moy; c'est ce qui plus le fait doloir."
     "Comment, Amours?"
Ce dist Raisons."Est ce dont de vos tours
Qu'il amera, sans avoir nul secours,
Celle qui a donné son cuer aillours?    1815
     Et qui vous sert,
Il n'a mie le loier qu'il dessert?
Certes, fols est qui a servir s'aert
Si fait maistre, quant son guerredon pert."
     Après ce fait        1820
Devers Amours, Loiauté se retrait,
Et dist einsi, que riens n'eüst meffait,
Se d'autel pain li eüst soupe fait.
     "N'il n'est raisons
Pour ce, s'il est vrais, loiaus, et preudons,   1825

1785. F conte--1816-9. These verses are found only in CEKJP.

78

For the reasons which you have heard.
　　　　And, to my satisfaction,　　　　　　　　1780
This knight has spoken of them very well,
Since I have found it all in writing here above,
And by reasoning has proved his contention.
　　　　Such is my opinion."
When Reason had related all her thought,　　　1785
Love spoke, who was very good-looking,
And gracious in manner and appearance,
　　　　And said: "Reason,
You have quite ably made your point.
And so I agree with it, except that it would be　1790
A grievous misdeed to rescue the lover's heart from its prison
　　　　Within the beautiful lady
For whom he feels the amorous spark.
So I wish him to love and serve her like one
From whom he's had much new happiness,　　　1795
　　　　For if he could
Live a thousand years and could serve her every day,
Never through service would he deserve
The great sweetness which she was wont to show him.
　　　　And if Pleasure,　　　　　　　　　　1800
Who has been the cause of many a strange alteration,
Makes him doubt his lady,
Must he be in despair for this?
　　　　Surely, not at all!
For in my service there are a hundred thousand yet　1805
Who love almost as strongly as does he,
And for it they have not the price of a whetstone.
　　　　And if I have the power
To cure him and bring him out of pain,
But he no longer has trust or hope　　　　　　1810
In me: then that's what makes him suffer most."
　　　　"How so, Love?"
Said Reason. "Is it then by your design
That he will love, without having any help,
The lady who has granted her heart elsewhere?　1815
　　　　And he who serves you,
He doesn't have in any way the reward which he deserves?
Surely, he's a fool who clings to serving
Such a master, when he loses his due."
　　　　After this　　　　　　　　　　　　1820
Loyalty drew herself up in front of Love
And spoke thus, that no misdeed would have been done,
If from such bread he had made a sop.
　　　　"And it's not right,
If he is true, loyal, and worthy,　　　　　　1825

Qu'il soit de ceuls qui batent les buissons
Dont li autre prennent les oisillons.
       Car se la dame,
Que je repren moult durement et blame--
Et c'est bien drois, car elle acuet grant blame      1830
De muance faire en la haute game--
       Premierement
N'eüst osté son cuer de cest amant,
Qui tous estoit en son commandement,
Amours, Amours, je parlasse autrement.      1835
       Mais sans doubtance,
Quant il l'aimme de toute sa puissance,
Et sans cause le met en oubliance,
Il doit dancier einsi comme elle dance,
       Nom pas qu'il face      1840
Chose de quoy il puist perdre ma grace;
Car s'il la laist, et ailleurs se pourchace,
Je ne tien pas qu'envers moy se mefface.
       Et si m'acort
Dou tout en tout de Raison a l'acort      1845
(Car elle fait bon et loial raport):
Que cils a droit, et ceste dame a tort."
       Et quant Juenesse,
Qui moult fu gaie et pleinne de leësse,
Et qui n'aconte a don, ne a promesse,      1850
Fors seulement que ses voloirs adresse,
       Ot escouté
Ce que Raisons ot dit et raconté
Et Loiauté, pou y a aconté,
Car moult pleinne fu de sa volenté,      1855
       Et dist en haut:
"Certes, Raison, vostre science faut,
Et Loiauté, sachiez, riens ne vous vaut.
Car cils amis, pour mal, ne pour assaut
       Qu'Amours li face,      1860
N'iert ja partis de la belle topasse
Qui de biauté et de douceur tout passe,
Et de fine colour; ja Dieu ne place
       Qu'il li aveingne
Que ja d'amer la belle se refreingne?      1865
Car s'a present ne le vuet, ne n'adaingne,
Au moins l'aimme il, et son cuer la compaingne.
       Dont n'est ce assez?
Doit il estre de li amer lassez?
Certes, nennil! Car on n'est pas amez,      1870
Ne conjoïs toudis, n'amis clamez:
       Non est, sans doute.


1831. F fausse game--1858. DEKJ certes riens--1861-84. These
verses are found only in EKJR.

That he should be one of those who beat the bushes
From which others take the birds.
      For if the lady,
Whom I blame and condemn very harshly--
And that's quite right, for she draws to herself     1830
Great blame for proving fickle in this serious game--
      Had not
First taken her heart away from this lover,
Who was completely under her command,
Love, Love, I would have spoken differently.     1835
      But doubtlessly,
Since he loves her with all his power,
And she without cause forgets him,
He ought to dance the same as she does,
      Not that  he should do     1840
Any deed by which he might lose my favor;
But if he left her, and looked elsewhere,
I would not hold that he sinned against me.
      And so I concur
Completely with everything in Reason's resolution     1845
(For she has made a good and true account):
Namely that he is right, and this lady's wrong."  ·
      And when Youth,
Who was very gay and full of happiness,
And who pays no mind to gifts or promises,     1850
Except those her desire points toward,
      Had heard
What Reason had said and related
And also Loyalty, she thought little of it,
For she was very full of her own will,     1855
      And she said loudly:
"Surely, Reason, your wisdom fails,
And Loyalty, know this, nothing avails you,
For this lover, despite any pain, any assault
      That Love may inflict on him,     1860
Will never be parted from that beautiful topaz
Who in beauty and in sweetness surpasses all,
And in pure color; may it never please God
      For it to happen
That he ever refrains from loving that beauty!     1865
For if at present she doesn't want him, won't bend to him,
At least he loves her, and his heart accompanies her.
      And isn't this enough?
Must he be tired of loving her?
Surely, not! For no one's loved,     1870
Or treated courteously, or called lover every day:
      Without a doubt, it isn't so.

Raison, fols est amans qui vous escoute,
Ne qui ensuit vos dis, ne vostre route.
Et qui le fait, je di qu'il ne voit goute.                                    1875
          Et par ma foy,
Nous ferons tant, Amours, ma dame et moy,
Que son cuer yert si pris, et en tel ploy,
Que nuit, ne jour ne partira de soy.
          Ne vos effors,                                                       1880
Ne doubtez pas, ne sera ja si fors
Que li fins cuers de cest amant soit hors
De la trés belle ou po treuve confors.
          Qu'Amour, ma dame,
Qui son cuer art, teint, bruit, et enflame,                                   1885
Et moy qui sui encor a tout ma flame,
En ceste amour le tenrons; car, par m'ame,
          Il le couvient.
Et se des maus dolereus plus li vient
Qu'a la dame qui dalez lui se tient,                                          1890
Fors est assez; bien les porte et soustient."
          Lors s'avisa
Li gentils rois, et bonnement ris a
De Juenesse qui einsi devisa;                                        [21r]
Mais onques meins pour ce ne l'en prisa,                                      1895
          Qu'elle faisoit
Tout son devoir de ce qu'elle disoit,
Et de son vueil plus chier denrée avoit,
Que x. livres de son profit n'amoit.
          Si dist: "Juenesse,                                                 1900
Bele dame, vous estes grant maistresse
Qui cest amant tenez en grant destresse,
En povreté, en misere, en tristesse,
          Vous et Amours.
Vez que li las a perdu tout secours,*                                        1905
Ne ses cuers n'a refuge, ne recours,
Fors a la mort qui a li vient le cours.
          Car travillier
Le volez trop, et dou tout essillier.
Or a trouvé, s'il vous plaist, consillier                                    1910
Bon et loial; laissiez le consillier;
          Si ferez bien.
Car il est pris en si estroit lïen
Qu'il n'i scet tour d'eschaper, ne engien."
"Certes, sire, de ce ne faire rien.                                          1915
          Eins amera
La trés bele pour qui tant d'amer a.
Et, s'il y muert, chascuns le clamera
Martir d'amours, et honneur li sera,

1899. CBDEKJ auoit--1905. A Vees

82

Reason, that lover's a fool who listens to you,
Or who follows your dictates, or your path.
And whoever does so, I say he can't see a thing.          1875
            And by my faith,
We will do much, Love, my lady and I,
So that his heart will be so imprisoned, in such straits
That night or day it will not leave her.
            Nor will your efforts,                        1880
Don't doubt this, ever be forceful enough
That the pure heart of this lover will ever be outside
The very beautiful lady where it finds so little comfort.
            Thus Love, my lady,
Who burns, pales, scorches, and inflames his heart,      1885
And I, who am still in all my fire,
Will hold him in this love affair; for by my soul,
            It must be so.
And if more painful sickness comes to him
Than to the lady who is holding herself by his side,     1890
His power's sufficient; he bears and suffers it well."
            Then the noble king
Deliberated, and heartily laughed at
Youth, who had spoken in such a way;
Even so he didn't prize her any less,                    1895
            Since she did
Her duty completely by saying what she did,
And he valued her wishes much more dearly
Than he loved ten pounds of his own profit.
            So he said: "Youth,                           1900
Beautiful lady, you are the great mistress
Who keeps this lover in such great distress,
In poverty, in misery, in sadness,
            You and Love.
You see that this weary one has lost all aid,            1905
Nor does his heart have refuge, or recourse,
Except to death who in time will come to him.
            But you would
Torture him too much, estrange him from everything.
Now he has found, if you please, a counselor            1910
Good and loyal; let her counsel him;
            Thus you'll do well.
For he is caught in so tight a place
That he knows no trick or scheme to escape from it."
"Surely, sire, I'll do nothing of the kind.             1915
            Instead he'll love
That great beauty for whose sake he has such bitterness,
And, if he dies from it, everyone will call him
A martyr for love, and this will be to his honor

                    S'il muert pour li."                    1920

Quant Juenesse ot son parler assevi,
Li rois parla a euls et dist einsi:
"Nous ne sommes pas assemblé ici
            Pour desputer
S'il doit amer sa dame ou non amer,                        1925
Mais pour savoir li quels a plus d'amer,
Et qui plus sent crueus les maus d'amer,
            Si com moy samble.
Or estes vous en acort tout ensamble
Que plus de mal en cest amant s'assamble               1930
Qu'en la dame; ne pas ne me dessamble
            De cest acort,
Einsois m'i tieng dou tout et m'i acort,
Que cils amans est plus long de confort
Que la dame ne soit, que Diex confort.                    1935
            Si en feray
Le jugement einsi com je saray,
Car tel chose pas acoustumé n'ay,
Et uns autres  vraiement, bien le say,
            Mieus le feroit.                                1940
Je di einsi--consideré a droit
L'entention de Raison ci endroit,
Et les raisons de vous qui volez droit,
            Et Loiauté
Qui en a dit la pure verité,                               1945
Ne n'i chasse barat ne fausseté,
D'Amours aussi qui en a bien parlé,
            Et de Juenesse--
Que cils amans sueffre plus de tristesse,
Et que li maus d'amours plus fort le blesse            1950
Que la dame, ou moult a de noblesse,
            Et que plus long
Est de confort, dont il ont bon besoing;
Et pour ce di mon jugement et doing
Qu'il a plus mal qu'elle n'a, plus de soing.           1955
            Et de grevance."


Quant li bons rois ot rendu sa sentence,
Dont par Raison fu faite l'ordenance,
Li chevaliers iluec, en sa presence,
            L'en mercia,                                     1960
Et, en pensant, la dame s'oublia
Si durement que nul mot dit n'i a.
Mais nompourquant en la fin ottria
            Qu'elle tenoit

If he does die for her sake."                              1920

When Youth had brought her speech to an end,
The king spoke to them and said thus:
"We are not assembled here
        To dispute
If he should love his lady or not,                         1925
But rather to know which has more unhappiness,
And which suffers more the cruel pangs of love,
        Or so it seems to me.
Now you all are in complete agreement
That more pain comes together in this lover               1930
Than in the lady; and in no way do I differ
        From this conclusion,
But support it firmly in every way and concur with it,
Namely that this lover is further from comfort
Than is this lady, may God console her.                    1935
        So in this matter I'll
Make a decision according to my understanding,
For I am not experienced in such matters.
And another truly, well I know it,
        Would do it better.                                1940
I say this--rightly considering
The opinion of Reason here herself,
And the arguments of you who wish for justice,
        And of Loyalty,
Who in this has told the pure truth,                       1945
Who doesn't resort to ruses or deception,
And also of Love, who has spoken skillfully here,
        And of Youth--
That this lover suffers more sadness,
And that the pains of love wound him more grievously       1950
Than the lady, in whom there's great nobility,
        And that he's much further
From comfort, of which he has real need;
And therefore I speak and render my judgment
That he has more hurt than she, more care,                 1955
        And more distress."

When the good king had given his decision,
Whose logic had been advanced by Reason,
The knight there, in his presence,
        Thanked him for it,                                1960
And, pensive, the lady forgot herself
So much that she uttered not a word.
But nonetheless in the end she granted
        That she would accept

Le jugement que li rois fait avoit,                     1965
Car si sages et si loiaus estoit
Qu'envers nelui fors raison ne feroit.
          Adont li rois
En sousriant les a pris par les dois
Et les assist seur le tapis norois,                     1970
Long des autres, si qu'il n'i ot qu'euls trois.
          Si leur enorte
Et deprie chascun qu'il se conforte,
Car se le cuer longuement tel mal porte,
Il en porroit mors estre, et elle morte               1975
          (Que ja n'aveingne);
Mais chascuns d'eaus bon corage reprengne,            *[21v]*
Car li cuers trop se destruit et mehaingne
Qui en tel plour et tel dolour se baingne;
          Et recorder                                   1980
Voit on souvent qu'on doit tout oublier
Ce qu'on voit bien qu'on ne puet amender,
Ne recouvrer par pleindre ne plourer.
          S'einsi le font,
Vers Loiauté, ce dit, pas ne meffont;                  1985
Mais s'en ce plour pour amer se meffont,
Homicides de leur ames se font
          Et de leur vie.
Après li rois appella sa maisnie;
Si vint Franchise, Honneur, et Courtoisie,             1990
Biauté, Desir, Leësse l'envoisie,
          Et Hardiesse,
Prouesse, Amour, Loiauté, et Largesse,
Voloir, Penser, Richesse, avec Juenesse,
Et puis Raison, qui de tous fu maistresse.             1995
          Si leur commande
Que chascuns d'eaus a honnourer entende
Ces .ij. amans, et qu'Amour leur deffende
Merencolie, après, que la viande
          Soit aprestée,                                2000
Car il estoit ja près de la vesprée;
Et il ont fait son vueil sans demourée,
Com bonne gent et bien endoctrinée.
          Lors se sont trait
Vers les amans, sans faire plus de plait,              2005
Et chascuns d'eaus a son pooir a fait
Ce qu'il pense qui leur agree et plait,
          Qu'entalenté
En estoient de bonne volenté.
Et li amant ont congié demandé,                        2010
Mais on leur a baudement refusé,

2009. FKJ lack En.

86

The judgment that the king had made,                    1965
For he was so wise and so loyal
That to no one would he do anything but what was right.
          Then the king,
Smiling, took them by the hand.
And seated them on the Norwegian rug,                   1970
Far from the others, so that there were only those three.
          And so he exhorted them
And begged each one to take comfort,
For if the heart should bear such a pain a long time,
He could die from it, and so could she                  1975
          (May it never happen);
Instead, they should each regain their senses,
For the heart destroys and maims itself too much
Which wallows in such weeping and pain.
          And one often                                  1980
Sees confirmed the view that all should be forgotten.
Which one sees that he can't better
Or recover by moaning and crying.
          And if they did so,
Toward Loyalty, he said, they'd commit no sin;          1985
But if in crying so for love they did wrong,
They made themselves the murderers of their own souls
          And of their lives.
Afterward the king summoned his court;
So Liberality, Honor, and Courtesy,                     1990
Beauty, Desire, mirthful Happiness,
          And Hardihood,
Prowess, Love, Loyalty, and Generosity,
Will, Thought, Wealth, along with Youth,
And then Reason came forward, who was mistress over all.
          And he requested them each
To strive to honor these two lovers,
And asked that Love fend off melancholy
From them, and, afterward, that a meal
          Be prepared,                                   2000
For it was then quite close to vespers;
And they accomplished his will without delay,
Like a retinue both good and well instructed.
          Then they drew up
Toward the lovers, without making any more discussion,  2005
And each of them did to the best of his ability
What he thought would please and suit them,
          For eager
They were to be of good will in this.
And the lovers asked to go,                             2010
But they were adamantly refused,

87

              Car Courtoisie,
Franchise, Honneur, et Largesse s'amie,
Li gentils rois, qui pas ne s'i oublie,
Et chascuns d'eaus moult durement les prie          2015
              De demourer.
Et il estoit près heure de souper,
Et a ce mot on prist l'iaue a corner
Par le chastel, et forment a tromper;
              Si se leverent,                        2020
Et .ij. et .ij. en la sale en alerent;
Après leurs mains courtoisement laverent;
Puis s'assirent, si burent et mengierent,
              Selonc raison,
Car il y ot planté et a foison                       2025
De quanqu'on puet dire n'avoir de bon.
Après mengier, les prist par le giron
              Li gentils rois
Et si leur dist: "Vous n'en irez des mois,
Car je vous vueil oster a ceste fois                 2030
Les pensées qui vous font moult d'anois."
              Le chevalier
Moult humblement l'en prist a mercier,
Et aussi fist la dame qui targier
Ne pooit plus, ce dit, de repairier.                 2035
              Et finalment
Li rois les tint viij. jours moult liement
Et au partir leur donna largement
Chevaus, harnois, joiaus, or, et argent.
              Si se partirent                         2040
Au chief de viij. jours et dou roy congié prirent,
Ou tant orent trouvé d'onneur qu'il dirent
Qu'ains si bon roy ne si gentil ne virent.
              Mais compaingnie
Leur fist Honneur; aussi fist Courtoisie,            2045
Juenesse, Amour, Richesse l'äaisie,
Et meint autre que nommer ne say mie.
              Car il monterent
Sus les chevaus et tant les convoierent
Que chascun d'eaus en son hostel menerent,           2050
Et puis au roy a Durbui retournerent.
              Ci fineray
Ma matiere, ne plus n'en rimeray;
Car autre part assez a rimer ay.
Mais en la fin de ce livret feray *                  2055
              Que qui savoir
Vorra mon nom et mon seurnom de voir,
Il le porra clerement percevoir


2015. CEJP doucement--2041. A au roy

                    For Courtesy,
Liberality, Honor, and Generosity his friend,
The noble king, who in no way forgot himself,
And each of them very earnestly begged them          2015
            To remain.
And it was nearly the dinner hour,
And at this word the call to wash was begun
Throughout the castle, and likewise loud trumpeting;
            So they rose,                               2020
And two by two went into the hall;
After this they politely washed their hands;
Then they sat down, and drank and ate
            In moderation,
For there was much in abundance                        2025
Of whatever one could either name or have that's good.
After eating, the noble king took them
            By the robe
And then spoke to them: "You'll not leave for a long time,
For I wish at this time to remove from you             2030
The thoughts that cause you so much grief."
            The knight
Quite humbly began to thank him for this,
And the lady did likewise, who could delay
No longer, she said, from returning.                   2035
            And in the end
The king kept them eight days quite happily
And at their departing gave them generously
Horses, harness, jewels, gold, and silver.
            Then they departed                          2040
At the end of eight days and took leave of the king,
In whom they had found so much honor that they said
They had never seen a king so good or so noble.
            And Honor
Accompanied them; and so did Courtesy,                 2045
Youth, Love, contented Wealth,
And many another whom I cannot name.
            For they mounted
Their horses and escorted them far enough
To lead each one back to his residence,                2050
And then returned to the king at Durbuy.
            Here I will end
My story; I'll rhyme no more of it.
But I have yet another part to rhyme.
For at the end of this little book I'll see to it       2055
            That whoever
Would like to know truly my name and surname
Will be able to recognize it clearly

En darrein ver dou livret et vëoir,
      Mais qu'il dessamble 2060
Les premieres vij. sillabes d'ensamble
Et les lettres d'autre guise rassamble,
Si que nulle n'en oublie ne emble.
      Einsi porra
Mon nom savoir qui savoir le vorra, 2065
Mais ja pour ce mieus ne m'en prisera.
Et nompourquant ja pour ce ne sera
      Que je ne soie
Loiaus amis, jolis, et pleins de joie,
Car se riens plus en ce monde n'avoie 2070
Fors ce que j'aim ma dame simplet et quoie
      Contre son gré,
Si ay j'assez, qu'Amours m'a honnouré
Et richement mon mal guerredonné,
Quant a ma dame einsi mon cuer donné 2075
      Ay a tous jours.
Et ce mon cuer conforte en ses dolours
Que, quant premiers senti les maus d'amours,
A gentil mal cuide humble secours.


Explicit le Jugement dou Roy de Behaingne.

In the last verse of the book and see it;
        Just let him remove 2060
The first seven syllables from the whole
And reassemble the letters in another fashion,
So that none's forgotten or hidden.
        In this way he'll be able
To learn my name, he who wishes to do so, 2065
Though never for this reason will he value me more.
And despite all this it will never happen
        That I'll not remain
A loyal lover, pleasant, and full of mirth,
For if in this world I had nothing more 2070
Than that I love my innocent and coy lady
        Against her will,
Then I've had enough, for Love has honored me
And richly rewarded my pain,
Since I've given my heart to my lady in this way 2075
        For all time;
And this comforts my heart in its misery,
Namely that, when first I felt the pangs of love,
I expected a humble relief for a noble ill.


Here ends The Judgment of the King of Bohemia.

27. Since, according to the lexicographers, *oci* is conventional onomatopoeia for the nightingale's cry, I have left it here untranslated. The word, however, could also be interpreted as the 2nd pers. sing. imp. of *ocire*. Cf. the following passage (directly dependent on Machaut's poem) from Christine de Pisan's *Le Livre du dit de Poissy*:

> Avoit atant
> De rossignolz en cellui lieu chantant,
> Qui ça et la aloient voletant,
> Qu'oncques je croy ensemble on n'en vid tant
> Comme il eut cy,
> Qui disoient: "ocy, ocy, ocy
> Le faulz jaloux, se il passe par cy
> Sans le prendre n'a pitié n'a mercy
> En no pourpris."

(ed. Roy, 176–84)

Although Machaut does not so obviously play on these double meanings, perhaps we should translate "kill."

55. The reading *embunchiez* of both MSS A and F appears to be a straightforward scribal error. I agree with Hoepffner in reading *embrunchiez* with the generally less reliable MSS K and J rather than *embuschez* with MSS B and R since the former readily explains, by simple processes of corruption, the readings of AF and BR and since we have no reason in this case to assume a later intervention of the poet.

61. The nominative form *qui* also gives satisfactory sense in this line: "and the lady who blamed her thoughts." The context, however, makes the objective form preferable since it is obvious that she is the victim of her grief and memories. The authority of MSS A and F, however, makes it possible that this change might be due to Machaut's intervention and not to common error.

147. The reading of AFMB can be understood as a simple diplography and must be corrected because of the meter.

194. The reading *nattendra* of DEKJP gives somewhat better sense and a closer rhyme. We cannot, however, discount Machaut intervention in a case such as this where the reading of AF is not a straightforward scribal error and cannot be rejected on other grounds.

246. The reading of AF in this line gives much better sense, and might therefore be an example of the poet's intervention.

262. The correlative *ne* does give satisfactory sense, since the young lover might well be imagined as being able to feel but not understand the experience of love. The divided authority of the principal MSS makes the choice of reading here difficult.

288. The preposition *de* gives a much clearer construction here and also makes that construction parallel with those in line 290.

301. I have retained the inflected past participle against the authority of the other MSS because such a form, though rare, is certainly not incorrect.

303. A's reading *blonc* does not give satisfactory sense and must be considered a scribal error.

421. Octavian's wealth and Galen's intelligence were conventional ideas in the Middle Ages.

543. The reading of FMC does make better sense here if we see Love as the source of either death or rescue, rather than, in the larger sense that the poem explores, a more complex phenomenon that promises both extremes of experience. Does the lady predict the lover's "double sorrow"? Or is she here merely noting the alternatives of reward and punishment she first mentions above (lines 529-30)? The divided authority of the principal MSS makes the choice difficult.

607. In the translation I have construed the lady as the implied subject of *faire*, but the construction is ambiguous and could equally be interpreted with the knight as subject. In this case translate: "but you must undertake a great and serious thing." Either reading gives satisfactory sense, but I have preferred the former since it ironically underlines her subsequent behavior in what *Raison* later correctly terms her *haute game* (1831).

733. The reading *voit monter* gives more satisfactory sense here, since one of the lover's main points is a vindication of Fortune's deterministic role and a subsequent assumption of responsibility for the misery he finds himself in (see lines 824-31). Therefore this change might well be due to Machaut's later intervention.

830. F's reading must be rejected because of the meter.

841. The reading *quanqui* of AFMC is best understood as a scribal error.

980-3. This is the first of four passages found in a number of MSS but not in A and F. See also lines 100-47; 1816-9; and 1861-84. Their cancellation from the latest version of the poem constitutes firm evidence of his continued interest in the revision of his earlier work. Though these passages should not be considered part of the text as it was finally constituted, I have printed them to clarify and exemplify Machaut's reworking of the poem. The text in each case represents, with some alterations of punctuation, Hoepffner's version.

1070. A's reading must be rejected because of the meter.

1078. The choice of forms is difficult here because of the divided authority of the principal MSS, but I have rejected the reading of A in favor of that offered by F and the other more reliable MSS.

1114. Hoepffner rejects the form *nuls* as an obvious error in flexion. In a composition of this date, however, such a procedure seems dubious.

1194-5. The translation of these lines is made difficult by the ambiguity of the impersonal constructions (no subject or object expressed for *aprendre* and *reprendre*) as well as by the wide range of meanings possible for these two verbs. The translation I offer is tentative, and it is certainly not the only one possible, simply the one I felt most likely in the context.

1233. The form *attrait*, found in all MSS, can be understood as a diplography. Hoepffner's emendation makes much better sense here, and I have retained it since it involves little more than an interpretation, prepositions and their objects being frequently run together in the principal MSS.

1265-6. Although the reversed order of these lines in A does not give an impossible reading, such a reversal clearly seems an error since the order as given in F and other MSS provides a less awkward construction.

1293ff. Hoepffner thinks this passage devoted to the praises of Jean of Bohemia and Luxembourg an *éloge pompeux*. The evidence of *Confort d'ami*, composed after Jean's death at Crécy, however, suggests that the narrator's evaluation of the king is not meant as exaggeration. Cf. the following passage from that later poem:

Il donnoit fiex, joiaus et terre,
Or, argent; riens ne retenoit
Fors l'onneur; ad ce tenoit,
Et il en avoit plus que nuls.
Des bons fu li mieudres tenus.
De son bien tous li cuers me rit,
Et pour ç'aussi qu'il me nourrit.
Il ne pooit estre lassez
De donner, et s'avoit assez
Toudis, quel que part qu'il venist.

Mais je te jur et te prommet
Qu'il estoit en si haut sommet
D'onneur qu'il n'avoit si haut homme
Voisin, ne l'empereur de Romme,
Que, s'il li vosist mouvoir guerre
Ou faire, qu'il ne l'alast querre
Tout eu milieu de son pais.    (*sic*--Read en?)
                        (ed. Hoepffner, 2930-9;
                                2975-81)

1326. A's reading here is possible as well, but I have
rejected it because it appears to be the result of a
scribal error (the omission of a nasal stroke) rather than
a correction.

1343. A's reading must be rejected because of the meter.

1366. Durbuy, one of Jean's favorite residences,
is now a small village in the Belgian section of
Luxembourg.

1440. The reading of A must be rejected as hypermetric.

1691. F's reading here gives better sense.

1742. The reading of AFMEKJ gives a very strained
sense since it requires an awkward change of subject.
I have treated it as a common scribal error and printed
*la* as in the other MSS.

1905. A's reading must be rejected because of the meter.

2055ff. The solution to the anagram contained, as
Machaut tells us, in the poem's last line is not straight-
forward. I quote from Hoepffner's interesting solution:

Das übliche *Guillaume de Machaut* lässt sich nich
daraus gewinnen; es fehlen dafur zwei Buchstaben,
*a* und *u*; zwei andere, *i* und *n*, bleiben übrig. Da

nun *Machaut* nicht geändert kann, so muss
man sie in *Guillaume* anzubringen suchen. Da bietet
sich nun das den Anforderungen genügende *Guillemin*.
Dass diese Namensform damals üblich war, zeigt
unter anderem ihr Vorkommen im *Combat des Trente*...
(Hoepffner 1906, p. 405)

Hoepffner's points are well taken. Once the required
letters are removed to spell the invariable form
*Machaut*, the ones which remain cannot spell *Guillaume*.
Thus Hoepffner proposes the well-attested by-form
*Guillemin* as a solution for the anagram. In his
article, he goes on to demonstrate that this same
form is necessary to solve the similar anagram that
closes Machaut's *Remède de Fortune*.

The following passages are cited to illustrate the source
relationship between Machaut's poem and Chaucer's *The Book of
the Duchess*. The list, in the main, derives from the work
done by Wimsatt and Kittredge (see the works cited in the
bibliography); I have, however, added several passages from
Chaucer that I believe may have their source, to a greater
or lesser degree, in Machaut. For convenience I have made two
lists. The first contains passages from Chaucer which are likely
to be directly dependent on Machaut; I have quoted the correspon-
ding lines in full. The second consists of passages which,
at the least, are paralleled by those in Machaut; here I have
given line correspondences only. Parallels I regard as doubtful
are followed by a question mark. All quotations are from
Robinson 1961.


I. Passages derived from *Le Jugement dou Roy de Behaingne*

1. 339-43 (*JB 13-14*)

   And eke the welken was so fair,--
   Blew, bryght, clere was the ayr,
   And ful attempre for sothe hyt was;
   For nother to cold nor hoot yt nas,
   Ne in al the welken was no clowde.

2. 388-97 (*JB 25-7; 1204-11*)

   And as I wente, ther cam by mee
   A whelp, that fauned me as I stood,
   That hadde yfolowed, and koude no good.
   Hyt com and crepte to me as lowe
   Ryght as hyt hadde me yknowe,
   Helde doun hys hed and joyned hys eres,
   And leyde al smothe doun hys heres.
   I wolde have kaught hyt, and anoon
   Hyt fledde, and was fro me goon;
   And I hym folwed, and hyt forth wente

3. 475-86 (*JB 193-201*)

   I have of sorwe so gret won
   That joye gete I never non,
   Now that I see my lady bryght,

Which I have loved with al my myght,
Is fro me ded and ys agoon.
Allas, deth, what ayleth the,
That thou noldest have taken me,
Whan thou toke my lady swete,
That was so fair, so fresh, so fre,
So good, that men may wel se
Of al goodnesse she had no mete!

4. 519-25 (*JB 70-4*)

He sayde, "I prey the, be not wroth.
I herde the not, to seyn the soth,
Ne I sawgh the not, syr, trewely."
"A, goode sir, no fors," quod y,
"I am ryght sory yif I have ought
Destroubled yow out of your thought.
Foryive me, yif I have mystake."

5. 526-8 (*JB 75-8*)

"Yis, th'amendes is lyght to make,"
Quod he, "for ther lyeth noon therto;
There ys nothyng myssayd nor do."

6. 532-3 (*JB 85-6*)?

And I saw that, and gan me aqueynte
With hym, and fond hym so tretable

7. 546-54 (*JB 87-92*)

But, sir, oo thyng wol ye here?
Me thynketh in gret sorowe I yow see.
But certes, sire, yif that yee
Wolde ought discure me youre woo,
I wolde, as wys God helpe me soo,
Amende hyt, yif I kan or may.
Ye mowe preve hyt be assay;
For, by my trouthe, to make yow hool,
I wol do al my power hool.

8. 645-6 (*JB 1072-4*)

Aboute, for hyt ys nothyng stable,
Now by the fire, now at table;

9. 648-9 (*JB 1078-80*)

> She ys pley of enchauntement,
> That semeth oon and ys not soo.

10. 749-52 (*JB 253-6*)

> "Blythely," quod he; "com sytte adoun!
> I telle the upon a condicioun
> That thou shalt hooly, with al thy wit,
> Doo thyn entent to herkene hit."

11. 759-63 (*JB 261-4*)

> "Syr," quod he, "sith first I kouthe
> Have any maner wyt fro youthe,
> Or kyndely understondyng
> To comprehende, in any thyng,
> What love was, in myn owne wyt,

12. 764-70 (*JB 125-33*)

> Dredeles, I have ever yit
> Be tributarye and yiven rente
> To Love, hooly with good entente,
> And throgh plesaunce become his thral
> With good wille, body, hert, and al.
> Al this I putte in his servage,
> As to my lord, and dide homage;

13. 771-6 (*JB 265-73*)

> And ful devoutly I prayed hym to,
> He shulde besette myn herte so
> That hyt plesance to hym were,
> And worship to my lady dere.
> And this was longe, and many a yer,
> Or that myn herte was set owher

14. 805-15 (*JB 281-5*)

> Hit happed that I cam on a day
> Into a place ther that I say,
> Trewly, the fayrest companye
> Of ladyes that evere man with yè
> Had seen togedres in oo place.
> Shal I clepe hyt hap other grace
> That broght me there? Nay, but Fortune,
> That ys to lyen ful commune,

The false trayteresse pervers!
God wolde I koude clepe hir wers!
For now she worcheth me ful woo

15. 817-29 (*JB 286-90*)

Among these ladyes thus echon,
Soth to seyen y sawgh oon
That was lyk noon of the route;
For I dar swere, without doute,
That as the someres sonne bryght
Ys fairer, clerer, and hath more lyght
Than any other planete in heven,
The moone, or the sterres seven,
For al the world so hadde she
Surmounted hem alle of beaute,
Of maner, and of comlynesse,
Of stature, and of wel set gladnesse,
Of goodlyhede so wel beseye--

16. 848-58 (*JB 297-30*)

I sawgh hyr daunce so comily,
Carole and synge so swetely,
Laughe and pleye so womanly,
And loke so debonairly,
So goodly speke and so frendly,
That, certes, y trowe that evermor
Nas seyn so blysful a tresor.
For every heer on hir hed,
Soth to seyne, hyt was not red,
Ne nouther yelowe, ne broun hyt nas,
Me thoghte most lyk gold hyt was.

17. 859-74 (*JB 312, 316, 318, 321-30*)

And whiche eyen my lady hadde!
Debonaire, goode, glade, and sadde,
Symple, of good mochel, noght to wyde.
Therto hir look nas not asyde,
Ne overthwert, but beset so wel
Hyt drew and took up, everydel,
Al that on hir gan beholde.
Hir eyen semed anoon she wolde
Have mercy; fooles wenden soo;
But hyt was never the rather doo.
Hyt nas no countrefeted thyng;
Hyt was hir owne pure lokyng

That the goddesse, dame Nature,
Had mad hem opene by mesure,
And close; for, were she never so glad,
Hyr lokynge was not foly sprad

18. 883-7 (*JB 331-5*)?

But many oon with hire lok she herte,
And that sat hyr ful lyte at herte,
For she knew nothyng of her thoght;
But whether she knew, or knew it nowght,
Algate she ne roughte of hem a stree!

19. 895-903 (*JB 292-6*)?

But which a visage had she thertoo!
Allas! myn herte ys wonder woo
That I ne kan discryven hyt!
Me lakketh both Englyssh and wit
For to undo hyt at the fulle;
And eke my spirites be so dulle
So gret a thyng for to devyse.
I have no wit that kan suffise
To comprehenden hir beaute.

20. 904-5 (*JB 356-8*)

But thus moche dar I sayn, that she
Was whit, rody, fressh, and lyvely hewed

21. 907-11 (*JB 397-403, 582*)

And negh hir face was alderbest;
For certes, Nature had swich lest
To make that fair, that trewly she
Was hir chef patron of beaute
And chef ensample of al hir werk,

22. 912-3 (*JB 411-4*)?

And moustre; for be hyt never so derk,
Me thynketh I se hir ever moo.

23. 918 (*JB 580-1*)

For hit was sad, symple, and benygne.

24. 939-47 (*JB 361-3*)

But swich a fairnesse of a nekke

Had that swete that boon nor brekke
Nas ther non sene that myssat.
Hyt was whit, smothe, streght, and pure flat,
Wythouten hole; or canel-boon,
As be semynge, had she noon.
Hyr throte, as I have now memorye,
Semed a round tour of yvoyre,
Of good gretnesse, and noght to gret.

25. 952-7 (*JB 364-77*)

Ryght faire shuldres and body long
She had, and armes, every lyth
Fattyssh, flesshy, not gret therwith;
Ryght white handes, and nayles rede,
Rounde brestes; and of good brede
Hyr hippes were, a streight flat bak.

26. 958-60 (*JB 380-3*)

I knew on hir noon other lak
That al hir lymmes nere pure sewynge
In as fer as I had knowynge.

27. 1035-41 (*JB 148-53, 156-61*)

Ryght on thys same, as I have seyd,
Was hooly al my love leyd;
For certes she was, that swete wif,
My suffisaunce, my lust, my lyf,
Myn hap, myn hele, and al my blesse,
My worldes welfare, and my goddesse,
And I hooly hires and everydel.

28. 1195-8 (*JB 461-2*)

I bethoghte me that Nature
Ne formed never in creature
So moche beaute, trewely,
And bounte, wythoute mercy.

29. 1258-67 (*JB 592-8*)

So hit befel, another yere,
I thoughte ones I wolde fonde
To do hire knowe and understonde
My woo; and she wel understod
That I ne wilned thyng but god,
And worship, and to kepe hir name

Over alle thyng, and drede hir shame,
And was so besy hyr to serve;
And pitee were I shulde sterve,
Syth that I wilned noon harm, ywis.

30. 1270 (*JB 641, 670*)

The noble yifte of hir mercy

31. 1275-8 (*JB 622-5*)

But if myn herte was ywaxe
Glad, that is no nede to axe!
As helpe me God, I was as blyve
Reysed, as fro deth to lyve

32. 1289-97 (*JB 166-76*)

Oure hertes wern so evene a payre,
That never nas that oon contrayre
To that other, for no woo.
For sothe, ylyche they suffred thoo
Oo blysse, and eke oo sorwe bothe;
Ylyche they were bothe glad and wrothe;
Al was us oon, withoute were.
And thus we lyved ful many a yere
So wel, I kan nat telle how.

II. Passages significantly paralleled in *Le Jugement dou Roy de Behaingne*

1. 37 (*JB 125-8*)?
2. 335-8 (*JB 15-9*)?
3. 368 (*JB 421*)?
4. 398-401 (*JB 28-31*)
5. 452-4 (*JB 50, 57-9*)?
6. 487-99 (*JB 206-15*)
7. 502-13 (*JB 56-69*)
8. 517-8 (*JB 59-60*)
9. 536-8 (*JB 86*)?
10. 555 (*JB 78-80*)?
11. 558-66 (*JB 93-101*)

12. 583-6 (*JB 195-8*)
13. 599-615 (*JB 177-87*)
14. 616 (*JB 1039*)?
15. 620-1 (*JB 684-5*)
16. 635 (*JB 732-4*)
17. 675-8 (*JB 729-40*)
18. 833-4 (*JB 394-5*)
19. 919-38 (*JB 340-7*)
20. 999-10005 (*JB 1246-51*)
21. 1056-74 (*JB 420-7*)
22. 1116-25 (*JB 1140-7*)
23. 1183-91 (*JB 453-6*)
24. 1192 (*JB 466*)
25. 1203-18 (*JB 467-76*)
26. 1219 (*JB 505*)
27. 1226-30 (*JB 656-8*)
28. 1236-8 (*JB 509-12*)?
29. 1239-44 (*JB 541-8*)?
30. 1271 (*JB 610*)